cocktail
CULTURE

cocktail
CULTURE

RECIPES & TECHNIQUES FROM BEHIND THE BAR
SHAWN SOOLE & NATE CAUDLE

TouchWood Editions
touchwoodeditions.com

LIBRARY AND ARCHIVES CANADA CATALOGUING IN PUBLICATION

Soole, Shawn, 1980–
Cocktail culture : recipes & techniques from
behind the bar / Shawn Soole, Nate Caudle.

Includes index.
Issued also in electronic formats.
ISBN 978-1-927129-94-4

1. Cocktails. 2. Bartending—Handbooks, manuals, etc.
3. Bars (Drinking establishments)—British Columbia—Victoria—
Guidebooks. I. Caudle, Nate, 1986– II. Title.

TX951.S66 2013   641.87'4   C2013-902064-0

Editor: Holland Gidney
Proofreader: Cailey Cavallin
Design: Pete Kohut
Cover and interior photos by Ron Green unless annotated.

 Canadian Patrimoine
Heritage canadien

 Canada Council Conseil des Arts
for the Arts du Canada

BRITISH COLUMBIA
ARTS COUNCIL

We gratefully acknowledge the financial support for our publishing activities
from the Government of Canada through the Canada Book Fund, Canada
Council for the Arts, and the province of British Columbia through the
British Columbia Arts Council and the Book Publishing Tax Credit.

MIX
Paper from
responsible sources
FSC® C016973
FSC
www.fsc.org

This book was produced using FSC®-certified, acid-free paper,
processed chlorine free and printed with soya-based inks.

1 2 3 4 5 17 16 15 14 13

PRINTED IN CHINA

First and foremost, this book is dedicated to my ladies, Jill and MG. You put up with my incessant need to be the best. And to the Vancouver Island crew of bartenders and geeks—you are the reason this all happened.

—Shawn Soole

This book is dedicated to the man who purchased my beloved video game collection for his son, so that I could afford to go to bar school.

—Nate Caudle

contents

ME DE
CAO

DISARONNO

IMPORTED·IMPORTÉ

K

LÚA

HERBSAINT

LÉGENDE
HERBSAINT
ORIGINAL

SPIRIT OF NEW ORLEANS

RBSAINT

PEMBERTON DISTILLERY
Absinthe

ARTEMISIA
DISTILLERIE ARTISANALE

La Clandestine
ABSINTHE
COUVET · SUISSE

VAL-DE-TRAVERS
700 ML   PAYS DE L'ABSINTHE
53% ALC/VOL.

La Fée

IMPORTED

La Fée

ABSINTHE PARISIENNE

BEST NEUTRAL SPIRITS DISTILLED WITH HERBS & SPICES
Based on an original 19th century recipe,
in association with the French Absinthe Museum.

(ARTEMISIA ABSINTHIUM)   50cL

PRODUCT OF FRANCE

P

cid

ABS

Forewords

Victoria was a surprise. I get to visit about thirty countries a year. I have been deported from countries that don't exist anymore, taken the night train from Krasnodar to Sochi, and flown to Australia for one day. Hell, I even once accidentally drank a glass of water, thinking it was gin. But nothing prepared me for Victoria.

Impossibly beautiful, it retains a whiff of the frontier, a soupçon of adventure and a sense of having to do it on your own, whether "it" is felling a tree, making cheese—or crafting cocktails. To see Shawn Soole in his adopted hometown forces even an Irishman like me to admit there may have been one or two advantages to the Commonwealth. Shawn and Nate, you see, *are* the cocktail scene in Victoria, as far as I am concerned. At Little Jumbo, they have created the hub, the incubator, the petri dish in which Victoria's passion for cocktails has multiplied wildly to infect local bars and liquor stores, private homes, and public events. There is no cocktail trend, no development, no twist or flourish that has happened anywhere in the world that Shawn and Nate have not learned everything about and shared at lightning speed with their guests, their colleagues, and their fellow bartenders. To be a regular of theirs over the course of a few months would equip you with a mixological education on par with that of any dedicated barhound haunting the finest places in London, New York, or Melbourne. I wonder if their guests, colleagues, and fellow Victoria bartenders know how lucky they are to have Shawn and Nate around? Experts who can open the whole world to them one drink at a time and gently guide them toward which technique or concept they should learn to appreciate first? Trust me—it's rare.

But there's something more than just knowledge, appreciation, and skill in the Victoria scene. In any given room full of cocktail aficionados—and more and more, that's *any* given room in Victoria—everyone always seems to be having fun. It's not the big city and it's all the better for it. (Having a large Australian around to bring you down to earth if you start putting on airs probably helps.) Victoria's residents seem to be simultaneously relaxed, excited, and always delighted to share a smile and a laugh—before asking you, in a serious tone, if you'll give them some honest feedback on the walnut-and-salt-caramel bitters they happen to be carrying in the side pocket of their cargo pants. This attitude extends beyond cocktails to Victoria's coffee and its food, the shops along the streets, and the restaurants clustered around the Inner Harbour. Everyone wants to make something with their hands and, while they're at it, to make the best damn thing they can. Reading this book is the next best thing to meeting these people. Shawn and Nate will guide you through the cocktail world of Victoria, telling you about their great friends and colleagues, sharing their passion for drinks, sliding you the recipes for some of their cocktails, and then passing along a few hints on how to make them. There are no better guides for the trip you're about to take. Just promise me you'll go to Victoria some day for real, all right?

—Philip Duff, Bar and Beverage Consultant

"Good things come in small packages" nicely describes the city of Victoria. It is a cute place, a quaint Canadian island town. Victoria is the smaller sister city to the bold and vibrant Vancouver. Not to be outdone, though, Victoria is a place where people have certain expectations about things—and, in my experience, they are seldom let down. In this case, the cliché is true: the better package is the smaller one, and it is Victoria.

The work involved and required to make a perfect cocktail—the painstaking effort and time spent researching recipes, creating your profile, refining your palate, and trusting in yourself and your skills to pull it off on a nightly basis—is a labour of love. That love often leads to perfection, which can be found in abundance in Victoria. This work ethic, or "code of the cocktail," has fallen on the shoulders of many and seems to be the collective responsibility of almost everyone I know who works in the hospitality and food and beverage industries in Victoria. And this most western of Canadian cities, with its penchant for mixological greatness, practises this good work each and every day.

Shawn Soole and Nate Caudle are at the forefront of a thriving, professional food and beverage fraternity that ranks as one of Canada's finest. Shawn and his team truly exemplify the code of the cocktail. It's more than a statement for them, it's a philosophy. And more than a job, it's a lifestyle. Shawn's meticulous approach to what he does, how he shares his passion and leads his team, and how he chooses to conduct himself are, quite frankly, what cause him to leap out of bed in the mornings—along with the never-ending joys of his wife and daughter . . . and the occasional drunk phone call from yours truly!

The reality is, because of many very committed, talented, and passionate individuals in Victoria, the good things are great, and the small packages on offer are exquisite cocktails built from a vast knowledge base and an appreciation of both history and forward-thinking. It's a vibrant scene that pulses in a way unto itself and ranks Victoria among the world's best cocktail cities.

In the end, it goes beyond the responsibility, and it goes beyond what's in the glass: It's not what Victoria bartenders *practise*, it's what they *live*. It's not what they offer, it's what Victoria offers them—which they, in turn, offer us!

The bar is open, so let's go have some cocktails!
                              —Kevin Brauch, *The Thirsty Traveler*

cocktail culture

It's a very special time for cocktails. There's a movement from around the world that's showing up in smaller cities such as Victoria. The foodie scene that has been building, growing, and evolving over the last few years has finally spilled over from the coffee, beer, and wine scenes into cocktails. Per capita, Victoria has one of the most densely populated restaurant scenes in North America, so it is only natural that the cocktail scene here be influenced by the high quality of food and drink this wonderful island produces and embraces.

Over the last five years, cocktails have taken a strong hold in our fair city—first with the vision of Solomon's (RIP, 2008–2010), and then with the introduction of bars like Veneto and Clive's Classic Lounge and the establishment of a specialized annual festival, Art of the Cocktail. With the foundation of the scene in place, more and more bartenders and at-home enthusiasts have slowly begun helping to create a world-class cocktail scene.

The industry here now boasts a whole selection of up-and-coming bartenders working their way through the ranks. A spattering of old dogs is leading the way, and, with the help of some great media coverage and accolades, Victoria is establishing a niche for itself as a cocktail hotspot. Case in point: some high-profile guests, including Philip Duff, Angus Winchester, and Jacob Briars, have come through our bars, hosting seminars and tutorials—and not just for professionals.

Yes, cocktail culture can't survive without cocktail enthusiasts and cities worldwide have some of the best that any bartender could ask for. The clientele in Victoria is second to none and one of the true reasons that the scene here is so fun right now. Their thirst for knowledge and the true "foodie" vibe that comes from them is incredible. We have regulars who make their own salt, bitters, and shrubs, the kind who hunt down hard-to-find spirits when they travel. Some of them are showcased in this book—and for good reason. They have become knowledgeable, independent bartenders in their own right. These home enthusiasts are amazing and represent everything that we stand for in Victoria's cocktail scene: family.

Little Jumbo, our place, is the latest addition to Victoria's cocktail scene. It has one of the most advanced bar programs in the country and will continue to grow and build the community that we have been for the last few years.

The great recipes in this book are the culmination of our careers along with contributions from some up-and-comers who are part of our fraternity. This book is about having fun, exploring what you know about cocktails, and pushing beyond where you thought you could take your palate.

This is a book by local bartenders for the global cocktail community to enjoy, learn from, and share.

Cheers, sláinte, prosit, and salud.

– Shawn Soole & Nate Caudle

the bartending basics

Like cooking, bartending is not a hard task; it's simply putting multiple ingredients together and balancing them out with various methods of emulsification. And all the techniques and methods you learn along the way help build and expand your knowledge of mixed drinks.

What follows are the basic outlines that we bartenders work within. In this industry, there are a lot of guidelines that can be stretched—or rewritten. That said, when it comes to the *basics* of bartending, there are some hard and fast rules.

Components

Bitters

Bitters are cocktail additives made from high-proof alcohol or glycerol infused with aromatics and flavoured with herbal essences. Dashes of different bitters can drastically change the drink you use them in. Most old-school recipes only call for three styles of bitters: Angostura aromatic, Peychaud's, and orange bitters, such as local Twisted & Bitter or Regans' Orange. These types, which are quite easy to find, are all you really need if you are a start-up home bartender. For professionals and enthusiasts, a wide array of bitters can be purchased these days. The Bitter Truth, Bittermens, and Fee Brothers are all good-quality, accessible bitters brands. If you want to foray into creating your own bitters at home, the blogs (p. 185–187) should be able to guide the way.

Ice

Hundreds of cocktail bloggers disagree when it comes to the necessity of specific ice in cocktails: some are pro while others are con. Either way, a good rule of thumb is to evolve with your surroundings. If you have horrible slushy ice, dilution will be quick as will chilling, so adapt to the situation and change your style. The "best" ice is solid, 1¼-inch (3.2 cm) cubes made by machines, such as Kold-Draft and Hoshizaki. For the home bartender, a standard ice cube tray will work just fine.

Juices

Juices are an important part of many cocktails. Whether they are citrus or more interesting kinds, such as pear, juices should be, for the most part, freshly squeezed. The fresher the better, especially when it comes to citrus. Fruit juice has a very short lifespan, as it begins to oxidize at a pretty steady rate from the moment you finish juicing. Some develop flavour changes while others change colour—citrus juice can lose its bite, while juice from pulpy fruits, like apples and pears, can brown.

If you can't squeeze your juice fresh and must pre-squeeze or use a packaged product, here are some hints: If you pre-squeeze citrus, know that it has about 6 to 8 hours before it is oxidized; pre-squeezed apple juice oxidizes much faster. If you buy packaged juice, look for one that's 100 percent juice, not from concentrate, and contains added citric acid. Citric acid is basically the essence of citrus juice concentrated and is an active preserving agent, akin to squeezing lemon juice over a banana to stop it from browning.

Liquors

Liquors are obviously essential to cocktails and come in myriad flavours, styles, colours, and prices. The cost, especially in BC, is somewhat important but does not necessarily indicate the quality of the product. When first buying a selection of spirits for home or your bar, keep in mind a few basics.

ANGOSTURA

AROMATIC BITTERS
AMERS AROMATIQUES

An aromatic preparation of
water, alcohol, gentian
natural flavours and colour.
45% alcohol by volume.
Un mélange aromatique
d'eau, d'alcool, de gentiane,
d'essences naturelles et
de colorant
45% d'alcool en volume.

100 ml

PRODUCT OF · PRODUIT DE
TRINIDAD & TOBAGO

For usage and recipe ideas visit our
website at: www.angosturabitters.com

Pour des idées de recettes et
d'emploi, visitez notre Web à
www.angosturabitters.com

PEYCHAUD'S

AROMATIC COCKTAIL BITTERS

DIPLOMA OF HONOR
AWARDED AT
GRAND EXHIBITION OF ALTONA-GERMANY

Bitters
equal for
cocktails
every bar
prominence

L'amer Peychaud
sur passe
om atique
les cock-
usage dans
meilleurs

GOLD MEDAL

NEW ORLEANS 1884-1885
BRONZE MEDAL ATLANTA, GA. 1895
GOLD MEDAL ST. LOUIS 1904 — GOLD MEDAL PORTLAND, ORE. 1905
HIGHEST AWARD, JAMESTOWN 1907

PRODUCED FROM
THE ORIGINAL FORMULA FOR
L. E. JUNG AND WOLFF CO.
803 JEFFERSON HWY. NEW ORLEANS, LA 70121
35% ALCOHOL BY VOLUME
CONTENTS 5 FL. OZS. (148 ml)

REGANS'

Orange Bitters
No 6

45% ALCOHOL
BY VOLUME

CONTENTS
(148ml)

NEW ORLEANS

Some things, such as amari, certain rums, and whiskies, simply can't be substituted; there are many recipes out there that specify particular brands, so keep that in mind. Do your brand research. Don't automatically go for an expensive brand thinking that it is a quality product. In this modern world of bartending, the price of a bottle of liquor now covers the bottle design, marketing campaign, and public relations. There are plenty of "bang for your buck" brands on the market that get overlooked because you never hear about them and their bottles are just plain ugly—but what matters most is the liquid inside. Finally, you should also consider *how* you are applying the spirit to the drinks you like. For example, don't use ultra-premium products if you like your drinks mixed with juice or cream; instead, use a nice mid-range product. The time when you should pick a premium product is when you are mixing a strong, spirit-forward drink that will showcase it.

In terms of selection, the spirits every bartender requires are a good vodka (Stolichnaya, Russian Standard, or 42 Below); a quality light rum and a quality dark rum (Havana Club or Flor de Caña do nicely); a Canadian rye whisky (Alberta Premium is one of those bang-for-your-buck brands and the only 100 percent rye available in Canada); a tequila (100 percent agave, such as el Jimador; choose a reposado, which is a little more versatile than a blanco); an old-school London dry gin for making G&Ts (Beefeater 24 or Tanqueray, though quality gins at a good price point are many); and finally, a Scotch whisky and a bourbon whiskey (head for a quality blended Scotch, such as Whyte & Mackay or The Famous Grouse, which will be not too smoky but plenty Scotchy, and for bourbon, pick up Maker's Mark or Bulleit).

To round out the aforementioned basic selection, add a sweet vermouth and a dry vermouth (Cinzano Rosso and Noilly Prat, respectively), and you'll have yourself the makings for a bank of cocktails that will keep you going for a few months. Once you have your base knowledge down, you can start expanding, maybe adding a bottle of Campari, Strega, or Chartreuse, which will further augment the range of drinks you can prepare.

Syrups

Syrups can be summed up with one rule: if you can only make it as good as but not better than you can buy it, buy it. (Why make falernum when you can order it locally from housemade.ca?) Homemade syrups should be made only in batches that suit your needs. For example, making a big batch of rhubarb syrup and only using a couple of ounces is nonsensical and will result in your batch fermenting and going off. Most syrups have a shelf life of 2 to 4 weeks before they start to lose flavour and turn. We have always found that with pulpy fruits, such as rhubarb or berries, it is best to freeze them before using them in syrups. The internal membranes break when the water expands, which makes it easier to extract the juice and flavour from the defrosted fruit.

Methods

Blending

Blending is constantly coming in and out of favour with bartenders around the world. Blenders have their place behind the bar and, in the right hands, can produce amazing cocktails—especially in the tiki realm of drinks. A blender is needed for recipes containing fruit or other ingredients that do not break down by shaking. Blending is an appropriate way of combining such ingredients with others to create a smooth, ready-to-serve mixture. When blended-drink recipes call for ice, you should use 1 scoop of ice per drink.

Modern blending, especially outside the tiki world, has been replaced by muddling.

Building

Building is one of the simplest methods of making a cocktail. Ingredients are poured over ice and gently stirred to combine their flavours. Drinks such as the Negroni and the Old Fashioned are classic built drinks. This method is one that's easy to do but hard to perfect.

Flaming

Flaming is where a cocktail or liquor is set alight, normally to enhance the flavour of a drink. It should only be attempted with caution and for the aforementioned reason, not to simply look cool.

Some liquors will ignite quite easily if their proof is high. Heating a small amount of the liquor in a spoon will cause the alcohol to collect at the top, which can then be easily lit. You can then pour it over the other prepared ingredients. For safety, don't add alcohol to ignited drinks, and don't leave them unattended. Light drinks where they pose no danger to anybody else, and ensure that no flammable objects can possibly come into contact with any flames from the drink. Finally, always extinguish a flaming drink before consuming it.

Muddling

Muddling is a relatively new addition to modern bartending, having only appeared in the last 10 to 15 years. To muddle, place fruits, herbs, and/or vegetables in a shaker and press them with a muddler. Doing so extracts their flavours, aromatics, and juices and also adds an interesting dimension to the drink that other methods don't produce. If you don't have a muddler, the handle of a rolling pin will suffice.

Rinsing/Spritzing

To rinse a glass, pour a very small amount of the desired liquid into the glass; swirl the glass until the entire inside is lightly coated with liquid. This method benefits the olfactory sense, enhancing what you smell while controlling how much of a certain flavour comes out in the drink. Though it

requires a special tool, the most effective way of rinsing is
to pour some of the liquid that you want to use into an atomizer and spray it into the inside of the glass. Doing so will
give you better coverage while using less liquid. Spritzing
is when you use an atomizer to coat both the inside and outside of the glass with a fine layer of liquid.

Shaking

When a drink contains eggs, fruit juices, or dairy, it is
necessary to shake the ingredients. Shaking is the method
where you use a cocktail shaker (see pp. 35, 37) to simultaneously emulsify and chill the cocktail. Shaking a shaker
is similar to a paint can being shaken at the hardware store:
the rotation, the shaking speed, and the ice combine all
the ingredients in such a way that they become a velvety,
balanced, and chilled cocktail.

There are three kinds of shaking. Dry shaking is shaking
without ice. This is done to emulsify the ingredients, par-
ticularly if the recipe calls for egg whites. Wet shaking is
shaking with ice. This is usually done after a good dry shake.
And finally hard shaking, a method made famous by many
a Japanese bartender, dictates a hard, point-to-point shake.
Put simply, shaking the shaker as hard as you possibly can.

Ice is key in the shaking process: your shaker should be
two-thirds full of quality ice cubes (see p. 13). Hold both ends
of the shaker tight. If you are using a Boston-style shaker,

hold the glass away from your guests so that if it explodes, which it can, the contents will spray all over you and not your guests. Shake hard; this is not a baby or a bag of chips. You should feel the shaker get cold and the contents change from heavy, clunky blocks of ice to more liquefied. When the shaker is almost too cold to hold, the drink is ready.

Stirring

Stirring is one of the most original methods of creating cocktails. It's simple and effective, yet somewhat difficult to master. The general rule is that anything spirit-forward should be stirred. Fill a mixing glass or tin two-thirds full of ice, add your ingredients, and stir with a good barspoon. Dilution and chilling are essential in a spirit-forward cocktail: too much dilution can ruin it, while not enough chilling means it will be warm. It takes some practice to get this balance perfect and to your taste, but it will become second nature once you have it down. You will need a Hawthorne or julep strainer (p. 36) to strain a stirred drink into your chosen glass.

Straining, Double-straining, and Dirty-straining

Straining has changed dramatically over the last 5 to 10 years. Some shakers, like the cobbler (p. 35), have built-in strainers, while others, like the Boston (p. 35) and Parisian (p. 37), do not and thus require the use of a Hawthorne or julep strainer (p. 36). In any case, straining removes large ice cubes, muddled fruit, and any larger, unwanted particles that may be unsavoury to your guests.

When it comes to double-straining, it's really a matter of personal preference, but the general rule of thumb is that drinks served in cocktail glasses should always be double-strained through a tea strainer or fine strainer, while drinks served on the rocks can be single-strained.

Dirty-straining isn't really straining at all. After you have shaken the drink, instead of straining it, you simply pour it into a clean glass. The Chivalrous Breakfast (p. 105) is the perfect example of a dirty-strained cocktail.

Garnishes

Decorating or garnishing a cocktail, especially in the modern cocktail world, can be done using just about anything but should always follow one rule: a garnish should *add* something to the drink. Whether it is a sprig of mint for olfactory purposes or a slice of lime to add acidity to the drink as you sip it, a garnish should always be purposeful. That said, it is important to avoid overpowering the drink. When garnishing with a slice of fruit, be careful with the size: too thin is flimsy while too thick can unbalance the look, and even the flavour, of the cocktail.

Citrus Peel Spiral

Use a parer or vegetable peeler to cut away the skin of a citrus fruit. Working in a circular motion, take care not to cut into the bitter pith.

Citrus Slice

One of the simplest, and most effective, garnishes is a thin slice of citrus (approximately 2 to 4 millimetres thick), which can be placed into the drink or, if you cut a slit in it, on the rim of the glass.

Citrus Twist

Cut a thin section of citrus fruit peel crosswise and then twist it. Serve on the side of a glass or in it.

Cocktail Picks

Picks come in all shapes, sizes, and materials these days, from cheap bamboo and wood all the way up to expensive, reusable stainless steel. They are perfect for spearing olives, cherries, or small fruit garnishes.

Freshly Ground Nutmeg or Cinnamon

You can use powdered nutmeg or cinnamon on your cocktails, but it is best to grind the spices fresh, using a plain or specialized grinder.

Frosting/Rimming

Margaritas and other mixed drinks often call for the rim of the glass to be coated with sugar, salt, or another powdered ingredient. The common method of frosting or rimming is to first rub the rim of the glass with a slice of citrus fruit, then dip the very edge of the rim into a small bowl of sugar or salt. Make sure that only the outside of the glass is rimmed—no one wants salt or too much sugar in their drink.

Maraschino Cherries

All bars have maraschino cherries, but since the cocktail garnish market is very lucrative these days, you can get quality cherries (not the radioactive ones!) from many delis and specialty food purveyors. Look for non-bright red ones.

An unnatural red colour is an unmistakable indicator of cherries that are chemically enhanced.

Sprigs

Sprigs of mint or similar herbs have always been popular in cocktails, but they are coming even more into vogue these days. With any herb, especially mint, it is best to use a nice-sized sprig and give it a spank (or slap): place the sprig into the palm of one hand and smack it with the back of your other hand. You can also gently scrunch the sprig in your hand. Doing so helps release the herb's essential oils and makes it an aromatic addition to the cocktail—and the first thing the customer will smell.

Zest

When, for example, a recipe calls for the "zest from 1 lime," or other citrus fruit, the entire skin is required. On the other hand, "2 lime zests" are two sections of lime peel cut using a vegetable peeler. You should never grate the peel because too much pith will come away with the skin. Flaming a zest (usually the thicker skin from a citrus fruit like an orange or a lemon) adds a different flavour to the drink. The explosive burst of flame that results when the citrus oils ignite creates a deep, clean citrus aroma and flavour.

Glassware

There are so many glasses in the world that every bartender drools over and every home bartender wants for
their collection. However, the basic three that you really
need for any bar are the "classics": an old-fashioned
glass, a highball glass, and a large cocktail glass (or the
unmentionable "martini" glass). Once you have stocked
up, the number of cocktails you can make grows exponen-
tially, and then you can concentrate on building the rest
of your collection. The other glassware listed in this section are more "luxury" items that can be procured later
on. Thrift and antique stores can be great sources for
finding that special little something for your collection.

Cocktail Glass—Large

This is where the infamous V-shaped "martini" glass comes
into play. Usually a larger glass (up to 12 ounces [350 mL]
at times), it can be found in pretty much every bar worldwide. Following the movement toward smaller glassware,
the large cocktail glass seems to be shrinking down to a
more appropriate size of 6 to 8 ounces (175–250 mL).

Cocktail Glass—Small

Said to have been modelled after Marie Antoinette's breasts, this small shallow coupe glass (also known as a coupette) is around 5 ounces (145 mL) and never larger than 6 ounces (175 mL). More suitable for cocktails that are spirit-forward and well chilled.

Fizz / Sour Glass

A slightly rarer find these days, this shorter glass is perfect for gin/rhubarb fizzes. It also accommodates most sours flawlessly, as well as any drink shaken over ice and then strained without, with room to spare for a splash of soda. Though the much taller slim fizz glass is an uncommon piece of glassware in most bars, it is a great substitute if you don't want to use the usual flute for sparkling cocktails.

Flip Glass

The flip is an interchangeable drink that can be served in a variety of glassware. We tend to use a vintage-style glass for aesthetics, but you can use tea cups, fizz glasses, etc.

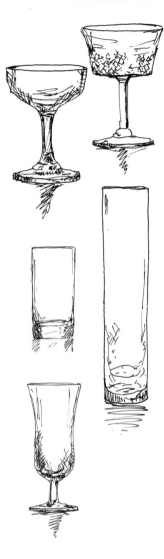

Flute

The champagne flute is synonymous with high lifestyle and fine drinking. The flute should be 5 ounces (145 mL), which is perfect for mixing sparkling cocktails like the Jessica Rabbit (p. 85).

Highball / Collins Glass

A classic highball is about 10 to 12 ounces (300–350 mL) and has a nice wide base. It's suitable for any highball cocktail or Collins.

Julep Mug

A julep mug is a very specific piece of glassware for the bar. Shaped like a tankard, it is usually made of pewter to conduct the cold of the crushed ice that is used in classic julep-style drinks. It holds approximately 8 to 10 ounces (250–300 mL).

Mason Jar

While they may sound highly irregular for cocktail glasses, jars make cheap, great glasses for summer patio entertaining and especially cool, trendy tiki drinks. And anything goes with regards to size and style, but try to stick with a wide mouth.

Old Fashioned / Rocks Glass

A classic short glass that you will see used in most bars for mixed drinks and straight spirits on the rocks. The standard old-fashioned glass is 6 to 8 ounces (175–250 mL), but nowadays you can get double rocks glasses that are closer to 10 to 12 ounces (300–350 mL).

Port Glass

A port glass is a small, wine-glass-shaped glass that holds about 2 to 4 ounces (60–120 mL). It can be used to serve most fortified wines, such as Madeira and sherry.

Snifter

The classic "brandy" snifter has begun sneaking onto cocktail menus worldwide. It can be used as an alternative to wine glasses or as an easier substitute for stemless wine glasses.

Special Coffee Mug

Hot toddy mugs or special coffee mugs are the relatively standard, heavy glass mugs you would normally get your Baileys coffee in. They are thicker than regular mugs to keep the heat of the drink in. A nog glass—an insulated glass mug or cup used for serving egg nog—is an acceptable alternative.

Tasting Glass

A smaller wine glass perfect for tasting spirits straight, trying a smaller pour of wine or beer, or having a spot of port or sherry. Tasting glasses can also be used as an alternative to traditional cocktail glasses. Bartenders are always looking for new ways to present their drinks and this glass is an increasingly popular choice.

Tiki Mug

These specialized, somewhat expensive ceramic mugs are moulded after various motifs of Polynesian tiki culture. They can range from 6 ounces (175 mL) to 12 ounces (350 mL).

Wine Glass

The wine glass comes in many sizes. During the birth of the bartending craft, it held only a few ounces but now balloons out to a monster 15 to 20 ounces (450–600 mL). An appropriate size for serving spritzers, coolers, or sangria is about 8 to 12 ounces (250–350 mL).

Wine Glass—Stemless

Self-explanatory: a wine glass with no stem. A bowl-shaped glass with a wide, flat base for stability. It looks great on a table with an ice globe, sugar rimmed, or with a nice, fat peel spiral hanging out of it.

Tools

We believe you can adapt to your surroundings and evolve your style to whatever you have on hand. For example, you should be able to make a good cocktail with nothing but a Mason jar and a teaspoon. But if you have access to great equipment, it will make your life so much better. The old adage that carpenters are only as good as their tools is very true for bartenders as well. However, the only tools you need at home to get started are a barspoon, some strainers, and a shaker tin. For bartenders wanting to build their collections, high-end barspoons, Japanese shakers, and jiggers are the next step—one that will showcase your personal style.

Bar Knife

A sharp knife about 4 to 8 inches (10–20 cm) long is the perfect length for everything from slicing citrus all the way up to dismantling a pineapple.

Barspoon

A simple tool that is actually extremely specialized. A regular parfait or long spoon is fine for at-home use, but for the professional, a twisted-neck barspoon is necessary. The twists should be tight and should stretch from the base to the top, where a small flat disk or muddler is very handy.

Boston Shaker

The simplest style of shaker: a two-piece shaker comprising a tin piece and a glass piece, although two tins have also become more popular in modern bartending. You build the drink in the pint-size glass, add ice with the tin half, tap, and shake. Takes a bit of practice to open, but it is the most versatile of all the shakers.

Channel Knife

An old-school tool that cuts a clean, crisp channel into citrus. It is useful for making thin twists, which are perfect for more subtle glasses, such as flutes, that require a longer citrus spiral.

Cobbler Shaker

One of the oldest and most common styles of shakers, this three-piece shaker has a built-in strainer. Sometimes the smallest cap section of the shaker is a jigger, used for measuring spirits on the go.

Hand Juicer

One of the most necessary pieces of equipment in the bar. There are two main sizes that you need: a yellow juicer for juicing lemons, limes, and oranges, and a larger orange juicer for grapefruits. These are pretty much the only sizes you need.

Hawthorne Strainer

The classic strainer that most bartenders have behind their bars, the Hawthorne has a tight spring around its perimeter. This makes it perfect to use with the tin portion of a Boston shaker for shaken cocktails.

Jigger

Standard Canadian jiggers come in 1 ounce (30 mL) and ½ ounce (15 mL) measures. The jiggers that we use are OXO measurers that have 5-millilitre increments marked up to 60 millilitres (2 oz). They are very accurate and can do fine measures.

Julep Strainer

Looking somewhat like a kitchen strainer or skimmer, the julep strainer has made a resurgence in cocktail culture in the last few years. It fits perfectly into the glass portion of a Boston shaker for stirred cocktails.

Muddler

The muddler was, until recently, a very important tool behind the bar; however, its popularity has slowly declined over the last few years. The best muddler for cocktails such as a Caipirinha is solid plastic or wood, moulded to the hands, and at least 10 to 12 inches (25–30 cm) long. It also sometimes has a teethed base.

Parisian Shaker

The latest trend on the cocktail scene, it's a slightly more cumbersome and complicated two-piece shaker that requires a certain level of skill to "crack" once chilled.

Peeler

A wide potato peeler is a perfect tool for every bar. It cuts perfect slices underneath the skin of citrus fruits without leaving any pith on the twists.

Tea Strainer / Double Strainer

When double-straining to remove pulp or ice shards, a fine tea strainer or "double strainer" is necessary. A simple tea strainer also works very well.

the recipes

In this section, you'll find more than 115 delicious cocktail recipes for a variety of skill levels. We have spent years developing and perfecting these recipes, and we are excited to share them with you at home. With everything from tikis to flips to new twists on old classics, you are sure to discover all kinds of drinks to love and share with friends. Speaking of which, we've also included recipes from our amazing friends—incredibly talented professional and home bartenders who share our enthusiasm for tasty and creative cocktails. Enjoy!

Drink-Making Difficulty

℣ **Easy**

Perfect for first-timers or for big cocktail parties. These drinks use liquor that is readily available. Relatively easy to make.

℣ ℣ **Medium**

For the cocktail nerd or home bartender who wants to build on their skills, these drinks use housemade syrups, liquors, and bitters that may need to be tracked down.

℣ ℣ ℣ **Difficult**

For experienced bartenders. These cocktails use more complex housemade syrups and extremely-hard-to-find ingredients. Tricky methods as well.

Classic-Inspired Drinks

We have a heavy grounding in the classics. You can make your own bitters and vermouths, smoke a cocktail, or create a flashy shrub, but at the end of the day, the classics should be learned, repeated, and perfected before you move on to your own creations. With that in mind, we've based some of these drinks on classic recipes with the same "Cocktail DNA."

Left to right: Saskatoon Julep, Humboldt, Cynar Crusta

Cynar Crusta ♈ ♈

Based on the recipe for a Crusta but substituting Cynar, an artichoke-based amaro from Italy, for the classic brandy. Doing so creates a drink with sweet, sour, and savoury elements that is finished with the sweetness of Aperol Sugar (p. 173).

1⅔ oz (50 mL) Cynar
¾ oz (22.5 mL) triple sec (Cointreau)
¼ oz (7.5 mL) maraschino liqueur (Luxardo)
¾ oz (22.5 mL) lemon juice
1 dash Peychaud's Bitters

GLASS Stemless wine glass, rimmed with Aperol Sugar (p. 173)
METHOD Shake ingredients with ice and double-strain into glass over fresh ice.
GARNISH Wide orange peel spiral

My Homie's Negroni ♈

GUEST BARTENDER J. ADAM BONNEAU

1 oz (30 mL) London dry gin (Tanqueray No. Ten)
¾ oz (22.5 mL) sweet vermouth (Cinzano Rosso)
½ oz (15 mL) Campari
¼ oz (7.5 mL) crème de cacao
3 dashes Fee Brothers' Aztec Chocolate Bitters

GLASS Old fashioned / Rocks
METHOD Stir all ingredients with ice and strain into glass over fresh ice.
GARNISH Wide orange twist

Morel Disposition ⅂ ⅂

GUEST BARTENDER SAMANTHA CASUGA

zest from 1 lemon
5 to 7 rosemary leaves
1 sugar cube
2 oz (60 mL) Morel Mushroom Infused Bourbon
    (p. 181)

GLASS Old fashioned / Rocks
METHOD Place lemon zest and rosemary
    leaves in glass with sugar cube, then pour in
    bourbon. Gently muddle until sugar is dis-
    solved. Top with ice cubes, add a splash of
    water, and stir gently.
GARNISH Lemon zest and rosemary sprig

Jalisco Sazerac ⅂

A relatively simple variation of the classic
Sazerac. Mixing quality reposado tequila, agave
syrup, and bitters makes a warming, deep-
sipping cocktail.

2 oz (60 mL) reposado tequila (Don Julio)
⅓ oz (10 mL) agave syrup
2 dashes Bitter Truth Jerry Thomas' Own
    Decanter Bitters
absinthe or Herbsaint, to rinse glass

GLASS Old fashioned / Rocks
METHOD In a mixing glass, stir tequila,
    agave, and bitters with ice and double-strain
    neat into absinthe-rinsed glass.

Angel's Halo ♈ ♈

GUEST BARTENDER J. ADAM BONNEAU

1½ oz (45 mL) Havana Club Rum
½ oz (15 mL) maraschino liqueur
¾ oz (22.5 mL) lemon juice
¾ oz (22.5 mL) Honey & Lemongrass Syrup
    (p. 179)
¾ oz (22.5 mL) egg white

GLASS Small cocktail glass
METHOD In a shaker, combine ingredients
    and dry-shake. Add ice and give shaker
    another shake so the mixture froths up
    nicely. Double-strain into glass.
GARNISH Lemon zest and a few smaller
    leaves from a lemon balm sprig

The Nymph's Reply 🍸 🍸
GUEST BARTENDER KATIE MCDONALD

1 oz (30 mL) Amaro Ramazzotti
½ oz (15 mL) falernum
Prosecco, to top

GLASS Large cocktail glass
METHOD Stir amaro and falernum with
    ice, then strain into glass and top up
    with Prosecco.
GARNISH Star anise

Humboldt ⍙ ⍙

A tongue-in-cheek cocktail based around Victoria starting to get areas or "boroughs" like in New York and other cities. We have Old Town and Chinatown, and now Humboldt Valley, where Clive's Classic Lounge is located. A variation on the Old Fashioned in lieu of a New York–style borough cocktail like the Manhattan or the Brooklyn.

⅓ oz (10 mL) Sugar Syrup (p. 183)
8 to 10 dashes House Made Chai Tea Bitters
2 oz (60 mL) Victoria Spirits Oaken Gin, divided

GLASS Old fashioned / Rocks
METHOD Pour syrup and bitters into glass. Add 6 to 7 ice cubes. Add 1 ounce (30 mL) gin. Stir with ice to dilute. Add another 6 to 7 ice cubes, then add remaining 1 ounce (30 mL) gin. Stir with ice to dilute.
GARNISH Lemon twist

Flower of Scotland ⍙

GUEST BARTENDER MACKENZIE WHEELER

1 oz (30 mL) Highland whisky
    (Glenfiddich 12 Year Old)
1 oz (30 mL) Giffard Ginger of the Indies
1 oz (30 mL) dry vermouth (Noilly Prat)
2 dashes Angostura Bitters

GLASS Large cocktail glass
METHOD Stir ingredients together and strain into glass.
GARNISH Lemon zest

Professor McHardy ⅄

GUEST BARTENDER STEPHEN QUIGLEY

2 oz (60 mL) overproof bourbon whiskey
(Knob Creek)
¼ oz (7.5 mL) South American Malbec wine
½ oz (15 mL) kirsch
2 dashes chocolate bitters
(Bitter Truth Xocolatl Mole Bitters)

GLASS Old fashioned / Rocks
METHOD Stir ingredients with ice, then strain
into glass over fresh ice.
GARNISH Orange twist (rub around edge of
glass and drop into glass)

Kilt in the Monastery ⅄ ⅄

One of Nate's earlier creations, this drink works
on multiple levels of flavour but keeps with
Nate's mantra that the real test of a bartender's
mettle is producing a good Scotch cocktail. You
can substitute Chartreuse Verte for the Elixir
Végétal, but Végétal creates the best flavour.

2 oz (60 mL) blended Scotch whisky
(Whyte & Mackay)
½ oz (15 mL) Amaro Montenegro
¼ oz (7.5 mL) Honey Syrup (p. 179)
1 dash Bitter Truth Lemon Bitters
Elixir Végétal, to rinse glass

GLASS Small cocktail glass
METHOD In a mixing glass, stir whisky, amaro,
syrup, and bitters with ice and double-strain
into Elixir Végétal–rinsed glass.

First Word ⅄

A skew on a Prohibition-era favourite. This drink takes one step to the left of the recipe for the Last Word, the Prohibition-era classic rediscovered by Murray Stenson, a famous Seattle bartender, formerly of the Zig Zag Café, now at Canon.

¾ oz (22.5 mL) reposado tequila (el Jimador)
¾ oz (22.5 mL) Esprit de June liqueur
¾ oz (22.5 mL) Yellow Chartreuse
¾ oz (22.5 mL) lemon juice

GLASS Large cocktail glass
METHOD Shake all ingredients with ice and double-strain into glass.
GARNISH Lemon slice

Dali ⅄

GUEST BARTENDER EMILY HENDERSON

1½ oz (45 mL) tequila blanco
¼ oz (7.5 mL) crème de cassis
¼ oz (7.5 mL) triple sec (Cointreau)
3 or 4 dashes Angostura Bitters
½ oz (15 mL) lime juice
1½ oz (45 mL) pineapple juice

GLASS Large cocktail glass
METHOD Shake ingredients together and double-strain into glass.

Around the World in a Kilt ∀

HOME BARTENDER JANICE MANSFIELD

1½ oz (45 mL) Arran Malt Fino Sherry
   Cask Whisky
½ oz (15 mL) Sortilège maple liqueur
1 oz (30 mL) pink grapefruit juice
4 dashes Angostura Bitters

GLASS Large cocktail glass
METHOD Shake ingredients with ice and
   double-strain into glass.
GARNISH Pink grapefruit twist

Chestnut Cabinet ⅌ ⅌ ⅌

GUEST BARTENDER JOSH BOUDREAU

Angostura Bitters, to spritz glass
Lamb's overproof rum, to spritz glass
1½ oz (45 mL) Jamaican rum
    (Appleton Estate V/X)
½ oz (15 mL) Giffard Chestnut Liqueur
½ oz (15 mL) dry vermouth (Noilly Prat)
3 dashes House Made Coffee Bitters

GLASS Large cocktail glass
METHOD Pour a 50-50 blend of
    Angostura Bitters and Lamb's overproof
    rum into an atomizer. Spray mixture
    through an open flame, coating a room-
    temperature glass inside and out, until
    it is tinted a brilliant reddish brown.
    Stir remaining ingredients with ice and
    double-strain into glass.

Managua ℨ ℨ

The Toronto Cocktail is one of the most under-rated and delicious true Canadian cocktails. This South American variation is named after the capital of Nicaragua. Using the same proportions as the classic Toronto, we've added a strong rum backbone.

2 oz (60 mL) añejo rum
  (Flor de Caña Grand Reserve 7 Year)
½ oz (15 mL) Amaro Averna
2 dashes Dr. Adam Elmegirab's Boker's Bitters

GLASS Small cocktail glass
METHOD Stir ingredients with ice and
  double-strain into glass.
GARNISH Flamed orange zest

The Harmony ℨ

GUEST BARTENDER KATIE MCDONALD

1 oz (30 mL) G'Vine Floraison Gin
1 oz (30 mL) Amaro Montenegro
1 oz (30 mL) sweet vermouth (Vya)

GLASS Large cocktail glass
METHOD Stir gin, amaro, and vermouth with
  ice and strain into glass.

Southern Belle ⅄

One of Nate's classic bourbon cocktails. If you love Manhattans, he'll move you to this drink, or to a Cocktail à la Louisiane. It has all the flavours that work well with bourbon and remind you of the South: peach, cherry, and the sweet nuttiness of amaretto.

2 oz (60 mL) bourbon whiskey (Bulleit Bourbon)
½ oz (15 mL) amaretto
½ oz (15 mL) Cherry Brandy (p. 174)
2 dashes Fee Brothers' Peach Bitters

GLASS Small cocktail glass
METHOD In a mixing glass, stir all ingredients with ice and double-strain into glass.
GARNISH Picked cherry

Paradisi ⅄ ⅄ ⅄

GUEST BARTENDER DIRK VANDERWAL

2 oz (60 mL) vodka (Grey Goose)
¾ oz (22.5 mL) Cardamom Syrup (p. 174)
3 oz (90 mL) pink grapefruit juice

GLASS Large cocktail glass
METHOD Shake ingredients with ice and double-strain into glass.
GARNISH Grapefruit twist with a few drops of House Made Chai Tea Bitters

Desperado ☿

GUEST BARTENDER SIMON OGDEN

2 oz (60 mL) reposado tequila (Herradura)
¾ oz (22.5 mL) Tuaca Liqueur
2 dashes Fee Brothers' Aztec Chocolate
    Bitters
absinthe, to spritz glass

GLASS Old fashioned / Rocks
METHOD Lightly stir tequila, Tuaca
    Liqueur, and bitters together with
    ice and double-strain into absinthe-
    spritzed glass.
GARNISH Flamed grapefruit zest

Le Chat Noir Dans Le Jardin (Rocco) ℣

GUEST BARTENDER SAMANTHA CASUGA

1 large fresh grape leaf, torn
1 sugar cube
2 or 3 fresh blackberries
2 oz (60 mL) dry vermouth (Noilly Pratt)
½ oz (15 mL) brandy

GLASS Julep mug

METHOD Muddle grape leaf and sugar
cube in glass until macerated. Break up
blackberries, then add to glass along
with vermouth and brandy. Top with
crushed ice and stir.

GARNISH Grape leaf, blackberry, and
powdered sugar

Gaudi ♼

GUEST BARTENDER EMILY HENDERSON

3 slices cucumber
3 or 4 fresh mint leaves
2 wedges lemon
1½ oz (45 mL) gin
½ oz (15 mL) lychee liqueur (Giffard Lichi-Li)
1½ oz (45 mL) pink grapefruit juice

GLASS Large cocktail glass
METHOD Muddle cucumber, mint, and lemon.
   Add remaining ingredients, shake, and
   double-strain into glass.
GARNISH Cucumber slice

Mi Hija Lolita ♼

GUEST BARTENDER STEPHEN QUIGLEY

2 oz (60 mL) reposado tequila
¼ oz (7.5 mL) elderflower cordial
2 dashes Regans' Orange Bitters

GLASS Large cocktail glass
METHOD Shake tequila, cordial, and bitters
   with ice and double-strain into glass.
GARNISH Lime slice (twist over drink then
   discard)

Wax Poetic ♀

GUEST BARTENDER SIMON OGDEN

quarter of a pink grapefruit
2 oz (60 mL) bourbon whiskey (Maker's Mark)
¼ oz (7.5 mL) agave nectar
¼ oz (7.5 mL) lemon juice
3 dashes Peychaud's Bitters
½ oz (15 mL) egg white

GLASS Old fashioned / Rocks
METHOD Press grapefruit into shaker. Add
  remaining ingredients, shake with ice, and
  double-strain into glass over fresh ice.
GARNISH Flamed grapefruit zest (discard
  before serving)

Treacle de Lux ♀ ♀

GUEST BARTENDER SOLOMON SIEGEL

2 oz (60 mL) Trinidadian or Guatemalan rum
  (Zaya)
1 oz (30 mL) Pommeau de Normandie
2 dashes Elixir Végétal
2 dashes aromatic bitters (Bitter Truth)

GLASS Old fashioned / Rocks
METHOD Very briefly stir ingredients with
  ice, then double-strain into glass over a
  large ice globe.

The Amateur ꙮ
HOME BARTENDER DAVE KELSEY

3 small slices cucumber
3 to 5 fresh basil leaves
1½ oz (45 mL) bourbon whiskey
½ oz (15 mL) lemon juice
½ oz (15 mL) Sugar Syrup (p. 183)

GLASS Old fashioned / Rocks
METHOD In a shaker, muddle cucumber and basil. Add remaining ingredients, shake with ice, and double-strain into glass.
GARNISH 3 drops Angostura Bitters

From Loretto with Love ♈

GUEST BARTENDER KEN GIFFORD

2 oz (60 mL) bourbon whiskey
    (Maker's Mark)
⅔ oz (20 mL) peach liqueur
    (Giffard Crème de Pêche)
⅔ oz (20 mL) lemon juice
2 thumb-length slices fresh ginger
    (not too thick)
1 oz (30 mL) ginger beer (Reed's)
2 or 3 dashes Angostura Bitters
3 fresh mint leaves

GLASS Julep mug
METHOD Combine all ingredients and
    shake. Double-strain into glass over
    crushed ice.
GARNISH Slapped mint sprig

Angel 31 ♈

GUEST BARTENDER STEPHEN QUIGLEY

1½ oz (45 mL) London dry gin
   (Bombay Sapphire)
½ oz (15 mL) sweet vermouth (Cinzano Rosso)
2 dashes lemon bitters (Fee Brothers)
juice from half a pink grapefruit

GLASS Old fashioned / Rocks
METHOD In glass, build ingredients over ice.
GARNISH Lemon slice

High Jack ♈ ♈

GUEST BARTENDER JJ SKIDMORE

1½ oz (45 mL) bourbon whiskey
   (Basil Hayden's)
½ oz (15 mL) calvados
¼ oz (7.5 mL) lime juice
3 dashes Cinnamon Bitters (p. 174)

GLASS Large cocktail glass
METHOD Shake all ingredients with ice and
   double-strain into glass.
GARNISH Granny Smith apple slices

The Golden Age ♈ ♈ ♈

HOME BARTENDER SARAH SHEA

1½ oz (45 mL) Ransom Old Tom Gin
¾ oz (22.5 mL) dry vermouth (Dolin)
¼ oz (7.5 mL) Cynar
¼ oz (7.5 mL) Sugar Syrup (p. 183)
¼ oz (7.5 mL) Yellow Chartreuse
3 dashes Dr. Adam Elmegirab's Boker's Bitters

GLASS Large cocktail glass
METHOD Stir ingredients with ice and
    double-strain into glass.
GARNISH Lemon peel spiral

Sarsaparilla Julep ♈ ♈ ♈

GUEST BARTENDER CYLE SERRA

handful mint leaves
2 oz (60 mL) bourbon whiskey (Maker's Mark)
1 oz (30 mL) Sarsaparilla Syrup (p. 182)

GLASS Julep mug
METHOD In mug, lightly muddle mint, then
    add remaining ingredients. Pack with
    crushed ice.
GARNISH Licorice root swizzle and dusting of
    powdered sassafras

Sarsaparilla Julep

West Coast Cocktail ⏝

GUEST BARTENDER SOLOMON SIEGEL

2 oz (60 mL) New Western dry gin
    (Victoria Gin)
¾ oz (22.5 mL) bianco vermouth
    (Martini & Rossi Bianco)
3 dashes Strega

GLASS Large cocktail glass
METHOD Stir ingredients with ice and
    strain into glass.
GARNISH Lox and applewood smoked
    cheddar

Italian Lighthouse Y

GUEST BARTENDER JJ SKIDMORE

1 oz (30 mL) Magellan Iris Flavored Gin
¾ oz (22.5 mL) Yellow Chartreuse
½ oz (15 mL) Cynar
3 dashes Angostura Orange Bitters

GLASS Highball / Collins
METHOD In glass, build gin, Chartreuse,
    Cynar, and bitters over ice.
GARNISH Candied orange peel spiral

Saskatoon Julep Y Y Y

Nate hails originally from Saskatoon and, like
any Prairie boy, he loves his Saskatoon berries.
We set about creating a Saskatoon berry liqueur
(p. 182) to use behind the bar, and this julep is
the tasty cocktail we created.

1½ oz (45 mL) Canadian whisky
    (Forty Creek Barrel Select)
1 oz (30 mL) Saskatoon Liqueur (p. 182)
½ oz (15 mL) Sugar Syrup (p. 183)
8 mint leaves

GLASS Old fashioned / Rocks
METHOD Place all ingredients in glass and
    let stand for about a minute. Add crushed
    ice, churn, then add more ice.
GARNISH Mint sprigs dusted with powdered
    sugar

Café Jalisco ⅂

GUEST BARTENDER CYLE SERRA

1½ oz (45 mL) reposado tequila
   (Sauza Hornitos)
½ oz (15 mL) Fernet-Branca
1 oz (30 mL) fresh espresso, chilled
2 dashes Bitter Truth Xocolatl Mole Bitters

GLASS Large cocktail glass
METHOD Shake ingredients with ice and
   double-strain into glass.
GARNISH 3 espresso beans

The Heartland ⅂

GUEST BARTENDER SOLOMON SIEGEL

1 oz (30 mL) Plymouth Gin
½ oz (15 mL) Amaro Montenegro
½ oz (15 mL) pear liqueur (Giffard)
½ oz (15 mL) lemon juice
2 dashes grapefruit bitters
champagne, to top

GLASS Flute
METHOD Stir gin, amaro, pear liqueur, lemon
   juice, and grapefruit bitters with ice. Double-
   strain into glass and top up with champagne.
GARNISH Lemon twist

The Heartland

Versailles Spice ℞ ℞ ℞
This cocktail was created for Art of the
Cocktail 2012. It is named after the town where
Woodford Reserve is distilled and is the epit-
ome of a spirit-forward autumn cocktail.

1⅔ oz (50 mL) bourbon whiskey
    (Woodford Reserve)
⅔ oz (20 mL) Cinnamon Smoked Madeira
    (p. 175)
⅓ oz (10 mL) Amaro Averna
2 dashes Amargo Chuncho Peruvian Bitters

GLASS Small cocktail glass
METHOD Stir ingredients with ice and strain
    into glass.

Tears of Ra ᛉ

Nate's homage to the Egyptian god Ra. It is said that the tears of Ra would hit the desert sand and bees would emerge. Tying the mead from the local meadery into an Adonis-style cocktail was the perfect meshing. The mead has a somewhat Lillet Blanc or Fino Sherry quality.

2 oz (60 mL) metheglin mead
    (Tugwell Creek Solstice)
½ oz (15 mL) dry vermouth (Noilly Prat)
½ oz (15 mL) sweet vermouth (Punt e Mes)
1 dash Regans' Orange Bitters

GLASS Small cocktail glass
METHOD Stir ingredients with ice and strain
    into glass.
GARNISH Orange twist

Drunk Uncle ᛉ

If you look at the "Negroni" family, you can of course include the Negroni, the Old Pal, and the Boulevardier in the same relative DNA. This is Shawn's take on the family—the outcast, the abusive one, the Drunk Uncle.

1½ oz (45 mL) Islay whisky
¾ oz (22.5 mL) bianco vermouth
    (Martini Bianco)
¾ oz (22.5 mL) Cynar

GLASS Small cocktail glass
METHOD Stir whisky, vermouth, and Cynar
    with ice and strain into glass.
GARNISH Grapefruit twist

Tiki Drinks

Every summer we do a kitschy-cool tiki party to launch
our summer cocktail menu. We love tiki—it's a style
that is quite hard to master and work with, but we have
tried to push the envelope by introducing "anti-tiki."
Anti-tiki is taking the makeup of a tiki drink and using
an ingredient that shouldn't be there, like amaro or an
interesting syrup.

Tar Pit

Tar Pit ♈ ♈

The epitome of anti-tiki, this drink uses Fernet-Branca along with typical tiki ingredients, such as rum, orgeat syrup, and pimento dram.

1 oz (30 mL) dark or black rum
    (Gosling's Black Seal)
1 oz (30 mL) Demerara rum (Lemon Hart)
1 oz (30 mL) Fernet-Branca
½ oz (15 mL) orgeat syrup (Giffard)
½ oz (15 mL) House Made Pimento Dram
1 oz (30 mL) lime juice

GLASS Mason jar
METHOD Shake ingredients with ice and
    double-strain into jar over fresh ice.
GARNISH Mint sprig and lime slice

Valdes Island Canoe Club Cocktail ♈
HOME BARTENDER BRUCE GILLESPIE

1¾ oz (52.5 mL) Jamaican rum
    (Appleton Estate V/X)
¼ oz (7.5 mL) lime juice
¼ oz (7.5 mL) lemon juice
¼ oz (7.5 mL) triple sec (Cointreau)
¼ oz (7.5 mL) House Made Falernum
agave syrup, to balance/sweeten the citrus
Alizé Red Passion, for float

GLASS Old fashioned / Rocks
METHOD Combine rum, juices, triple sec,
    and falernum. Add agave syrup until pre-
    ferred sweetness is achieved. Shake with
    ice and strain into glass over fresh ice.
    Pour a float of Alizé Red Passion for colour
    and sweetness.

Lazimon's Sorrel Rum Punch ♈ ♈ ♈

A simpler version of sorrel punch, where ground cloves, ginger, cinnamon, and sorrels (a type of hibiscus) are made into a syrup that's mixed with water for kids. Of course, adults add alcohol. Named for the Lazy Man.

1½ oz (45 mL) 151 proof rum
    (Bacardi 151° or Wray & Nephew)
½ oz (15 mL) Giffard Ginger of the Indies
⅓ oz (10 mL) Clove Syrup (p. 175)
⅓ oz (10 mL) Cinnamon Syrup (p. 175)
⅔ oz (20 mL) Hibiscus Liqueur (p. 179)
1 oz (30 mL) lime juice

GLASS Tiki mug
METHOD Shake ingredients with ice and double-strain into mug over crushed ice.
GARNISH Preserved hibiscus flower and umbrella

The Velvet Underground ♈ ♈

HOME BARTENDER JANICE MANSFIELD

¾ oz (22.5 mL) blackstrap rum
    (Cruzan Black Strap)
¾ oz (22.5 mL) Guyana rum
    (El Dorado 15 Year Old)
¾ oz (22.5 mL) dark rum (Gosling's Black Seal)
¾ oz (22.5 mL) Green Chartreuse
1 tsp (5 mL) Gomme Syrup (p. 178)
1 tsp (5 mL) Bottlegreen Elderflower Cordial
4 dashes Bitter Truth Jerry Thomas' Own Decanter Bitters

GLASS Large cocktail glass
METHOD Stir all ingredients with ice and strain into glass.
GARNISH Orange twist

Holy Hand Grenade ⅄ Ⅴ

Its unusual and eclectic composition is what makes Nate's anti-tiki Holy Hand Grenade a big splash. The name is a tribute to the Chartreuse logo, which may remind you of two things: If you are a little older, you will probably pick up on the Monty Python reference. For younger drinkers, it may remind you of a secret weapon in the PC game *Worms*. Either way, it's delicious.

1⅔ oz (50 mL) bourbon whiskey
  (Bulleit Bourbon)
1 oz (30 mL) Green Chartreuse
⅔ oz (20 mL) Apfelkorn apple schnapps
⅔ oz (20 mL) Giffard Chestnut Syrup
⅔ oz (20 mL) lime juice

GLASS Stemless wine glass
METHOD Shake ingredients with ice and
  double-strain into glass over crushed ice.
GARNISH Pineapple frond cross

Cannibal's Campfire Y Y

The Cannibal's Campfire builds into tiki a big trend in the industry right now: smoke. Smoky whisky goes great with Earl Grey tea and grapefruit. Add rum as a backbone and you have a simple yet delicious tiki drink.

2 oz (60 mL) gold rum (Mount Gay)
½ oz (15 mL) Islay whisky (McClelland's)
1 oz (30 mL) Earl Grey Tea Syrup (p. 176)
1 oz (30 mL) grapefruit juice

GLASS Tiki mug
METHOD Shake ingredients with ice and
    double-strain into mug over crushed ice.
GARNISH Grapefruit twist and charred
    swizzle stick

Good Ju Ju ♉ ♉

The true definition of classic tiki, this cocktail got its name from all the components being very traditional tiki: strong rum and sweet flavours, finished with pineapple juice. Sweet, spicy, and with a big kick of rum, it's all good juju.

1 oz (30 mL) spiced rum (Cruzan 9 Spiced)
1 oz (30 mL) gold rum (Appleton Estate V/X)
1 oz (30 mL) amaretto
1 oz (30 mL) Spiced Syrup (p. 183)
1 oz (30 mL) pineapple juice

GLASS Tiki mug
METHOD Shake ingredients with ice and double-strain into mug over crushed ice.
GARNISH Pineapple fronds and lime slice

Jamaican Switch ♉ ♉ ♉

A tiki drink constructed to showcase the ginger and molasses flavour profile of Switchel (p. 183), which is a very inexpensive mixer and great for hot weather.

1⅔ oz (50 mL) gold rum (Appleton Estate V/X)
⅓ oz (10 mL) Bornholmer Bitter
½ oz (15 mL) Sugar Syrup (p. 183)
2 oz (60 mL) Switchel (p. 183)
½ oz (15 mL) lemon juice
¾ oz (22.5 mL) pineapple juice

GLASS Tiki mug
METHOD Shake ingredients with ice and double-strain into mug over crushed ice.
GARNISH Pineapple fronds and lemon slice

Weird, Experimental & Mainstays

These are our greatest hits: weird cocktails that got us into the *New York Times*, experimental concoctions that we showcase weekly, and the mainstays that are some of our guests' favourites.

Bellucci

Bellucci ᵧ ᵧ ᵧ

Named after the actress, Monica Bellucci, this cocktail meshes the Angus Winchester Negroni (a fortified classic Negroni) with an Aperol Spritz Foam (p. 173). It's voluptuous, sexy, and screams "Italy."

2 oz (60 mL) London dry gin (Tanqueray)
1 oz (30 mL) Campari
1 oz (30 mL) sweet vermouth
     (Martini & Rossi Rosso)
Aperol Spritz Foam (p. 173), to top

GLASS Large cocktail glass
METHOD Stir gin, Campari, and vermouth with ice and strain into glass. Top with Aperol Spritz Foam.

Maria Full of Grace ᵧ ᵧ

GUEST BARTENDER JOSH BOUDREAU

2 sprigs fresh thyme
¼ oz (7.5 mL) absinthe (Lucid)
2 oz (60 mL) tequila blanco (el Jimador)
½ oz (15 mL) passion fruit liqueur (Giffard)
½ oz (15 mL) lemon juice

GLASS Old fashioned / Rocks
METHOD Place thyme and absinthe in glass and ignite. In a mixing glass, stir remaining ingredients with ice. Pour tequila mixture (including ice) into flaming glass and give drink a quick stir.
GARNISH Charred thyme

Cold Night In ♈ ♈ ♈

Clive's big break in 2011, this drink was featured in the *New York Times* and is one of the most over-publicized cocktails ever to come out of the bar. We were talking about fat washing one day, and no one had ever done grilled cheese before, so we did. It just happened that a *NY Times* writer was in the bar at the time, and the sensation afterwards was spectacular.

4 cherry tomatoes, roasted
4 basil leaves
pinch of salt and pepper
2 oz (60 mL) Grilled Cheese Washed Mount Gay Rum (p. 179)
½ oz (15 mL) Lillet Blanc
1 dash Bitter Truth Celery Bitters

GLASS Small cocktail glass
METHOD In a mixing glass, muddle tomatoes, basil, salt, and pepper. Add remaining ingredients and stir with ice, then double-strain into glass.
GARNISH Picked basil-wrapped cherry tomato and 5 drops Islay whisky

Sevilla Sunrise ♈ ♈

GUEST BARTENDER BROOKE LEVIE

1½ oz (45 mL) tequila blanco
1 oz (30 mL) Fino Sherry
½ oz (15 mL) orange marmalade
1 oz (30 mL) orange juice
½ oz (15 mL) lime juice
⅓ oz (10 mL) pomegranate syrup
3 dashes Fee Brothers' Aztec Chocolate Bitters

GLASS Highball / Collins
METHOD Shake ingredients with ice and strain into glass over fresh ice.
GARNISH Orange twist

Dawn's Reward ᵞ ᵞ

GUEST BARTENDER BRENDAN BREWSTER

handful basil, slapped
3 strawberries, hulled and quartered
1 oz (30 mL) dark or Jamaican rum
1 oz (30 mL) Spanish brandy
¾ oz (22.5 mL) lemon juice
½ oz (15 mL) Honey Tea Ginger Syrup
    (p. 179)
1 dash aromatic bitters
spicy ginger beer, to top

GLASS Highball / Collins
METHOD In a mixing glass, muddle basil
    and strawberries. Add rum and brandy,
    followed by lemon juice, syrup, and bit-
    ters. Shake with ice, double-strain into
    glass, and top up with ginger beer.
GARNISH Strawberry and basil sprig

Mayahuel Flame ♈ ♈ ♈

This drink was created for a cocktail competition in Vancouver. It got panned by the judges. They hated it, but it is now one of the top sellers at Clive's. It combines simple methodology with unique ingredients mainly made at the bar.

2 oz (60 mL) reposado tequila (el Jimador)
½ oz (15 mL) Green Tea & Serrano Chili
    Amaro (p. 178)
⅔ oz (20 mL) Ginger & Honey Shrub
    (p. 177)
⅔ oz (20 mL) grapefruit juice

GLASS Stemless wine glass / Old fashioned
METHOD Shake ingredients with ice and
    double-strain into glass over an ice globe.
GARNISH Wide grapefruit twist

Centennial 🍸🍸

GUEST BARTENDER DIRK VANDERWAL

1 oz (30 mL) London dry gin (Bombay Sapphire)
½ oz (15 mL) bianco vermouth (Lillet Blanc)
½ oz (15 mL) Hpnotiq
½ oz (15 mL) Sugar Syrup (p. 183)
8 dashes House Made Grapefruit Bitters
juice from a quarter of a lemon

GLASS Large cocktail glass
METHOD Shake all ingredients with ice and double-strain into glass.
GARNISH Wide lemon twist

Albino Hemingway Daiquiri 🍸🍸🍸

Developed after we were given some acid phosphate by Darcy O'Neil of Extinct Chemical Co. and Art of Drink, a cocktail blog. Most bartenders have been playing with the soda fountain concept, and we went about creating completely clear cocktails—albino, if you will.

2 oz (60 mL) white rum (Havana Club Añejo Blanco)
⅓ oz (10 mL) maraschino liqueur (Luxardo)
⅓ oz (10 mL) Clarified Lime Peel Syrup (p. 175)
¼ oz (7.5 mL) Extinct Chemical Co. acid phosphate
2 dashes House Made Grapefruit Bitters

GLASS Small cocktail glass
METHOD Stir ingredients with ice and double-strain into glass.
GARNISH Cherry

Rhubarb Fizz ℽ ℽ

A simple variation of a Pisco Sour. What can we say, it was summer and we love pisco. For the geeks out there, it's actually more of a Rickey than a fizz.

2 oz (60 mL) pisco (Capel)
⅔ oz (20 mL) Rhubarb Syrup (p. 182)
⅔ oz (20 mL) lime juice
2 dashes Fee Brothers' Rhubarb Bitters
soda, to top

GLASS Fizz glass
METHOD Shake pisco, syrup, lime juice, and bitters with ice and double-strain into glass. Top up with soda.
GARNISH Lime slice

Satchmo ℽ ℽ ℽ

GUEST BARTENDER J. ADAM BONNEAU

½ oz (15 mL) sweet vermouth (Punt e Mes)
⅓ oz (10 mL) crème de cassis
1 Tbsp (15 mL) Silk Road Japanese Sour Cherry green tea (dry tea leaves)
1 Tbsp (15 mL) Silk Road Spicy Mandarin black tea (dry tea leaves)
1½ oz (45 mL) overproof bourbon whiskey (Booker's 7 Year)
1 dash Angostura Bitters
1 tsp (5 mL) Silk Road Ceylon Gunpowder green tea (dry tea leaves)

GLASS Small cocktail glass
METHOD Combine vermouth and crème de cassis with Sour Cherry and Spicy Mandarin teas. Let sit for 30 minutes to infuse. Double-strain mixture to remove tea leaves. Pour into a shaker cup half full of ice. Add whiskey and bitters. Stir for about 10 seconds.

Double-strain into a sealable glass bottle. Pack Ceylon Gunpowder tea into the hopper of a PolyScience Smoking Gun and light. Let smoke bellow into the bottle for approximately 5 seconds. Seal bottle and give it two quick spins to smoke cocktail.

Pour cocktail into glass; give the bottle a quick little shake at the end, so that a bit of smoke sits on top of the cocktail.
GARNISH Orange twist

Satchmo

Roland Garros Y

Takes the best parts of British culture—
Pimm's and tennis—and combines them
with a French liqueur from Angers and
saffron gin from Dijon. The result is a
refreshing luxury-class gin and juice that's
colour is reminiscent of the clay at its
namesake French stadium.

1⅔ oz (50 mL) saffron gin
    (Gabriel Boudier, if available)
¾ oz (22.5 mL) Pimm's
⅔ oz (20 mL) peach liqueur (Giffard)
⅓ oz (10 mL) lemon juice
⅔ oz (20 mL) orange juice
sparkling wine, to top

GLASS Old fashioned / Rocks
METHOD Shake gin, Pimm's, peach
    liqueur, and juices with ice and double-
    strain into ice-filled glass. Top with
    sparkling wine.
GARNISH Orange twist and mint sprig

Faux Pomme Y

Nate's first actual cocktail to call his own. They say some of the best things in life happen by accident and this cocktail is no exception. While Nate was working at Solomon's, the then-chef asked for a nice, impromptu gin cocktail. He was later stunned by this drink's uncanny crisp green apple mouth feel, despite there being no inherent apple ingredients. The name was an easy choice thereafter.

1½ oz (45 mL) Plymouth Gin
½ oz (15 mL) Giffard Pear Liqueur
½ oz (15 mL) dry vermouth (Noilly Prat)
2 dashes Fee Brothers' Peach Bitters
sparkling wine, to top

GLASS Large cocktail glass
METHOD Stir gin, pear liqueur, vermouth, and bitters with ice and double-strain into glass. Top with a float of sparkling wine, preferably Prosecco.
GARNISH Lime twist

D'Vine Y

GUEST BARTENDER BROOKE LEVIE

1½ oz (45 mL) Viognier
    (or aromatic white wine of your choice)
¾ oz (22.5 mL) white rum (Havana Club)
¾ oz (22.5 mL) lychee liqueur
    (Giffard Lichi-Li)
½ oz (15 mL) lime juice

GLASS Large cocktail glass
METHOD Shake ingredients with ice and double-strain into glass.
GARNISH Orange twist

Italian Sour ⅄

A softer alternative for those who might
find a Negroni or a Boulevardier too aggres-
sive. But you have to like bitters a little to
enjoy this creamy pink concoction.

2 oz (60 mL) Campari
⅔ oz (20 mL) Strega
⅔ oz (20 mL) vanilla liqueur
    (Giffard Vanille de Madagascar)
1 oz (30 mL) lemon juice
1 fresh egg white

GLASS Old fashioned / Rocks
METHOD Hard-shake ingredients with
    ice and double-strain into glass.

Jessica Rabbit ♈ ♈

Originally an alternative to the French 75, this cocktail is quickly becoming one of our best sellers. Given that we cannot get Heering Cherry Liqueur here, we were forced to take an alternate route. A tall, slim-waisted cocktail that sparkles in red.

1½ oz (45 mL) Cherry Brandy (p. 174)
½ oz (15 mL) Apfelkorn apple schnapps
½ oz (15 mL) Giffard Ginger of the Indies
½ oz (15 mL) lemon juice
2 dashes Fee Brothers' Cranberry Bitters

GLASS Slim fizz glass / Flute
METHOD In a Perlini shaker, pour all
    ingredients over ice. Carbonate and then
    double-strain into glass.
GARNISH Channelled lemon twist

Tree de Vie ＹＹＹ

GUEST BARTENDER CYLE SERRA

1 oz (30 mL) Victoria Spirits Oaken Gin
½ oz (15 mL) Jamaican rum
    (Appleton Estate Reserve)
½ oz (15 mL) Sortilège maple liqueur
5 dashes Grand Fir Tincture (p. 178)
1 dash Fee Brothers' Whiskey Barrel-Aged
    Bitters

GLASS Large cocktail glass
METHOD Stir ingredients with ice and strain
    into glass.
GARNISH Orange peel spiral

el Greco Ｙ

GUEST BARTENDER EMILY HENDERSON

3 or 4 fresh basil leaves
2 wedges lemon
crack of fresh black pepper
½ oz (15 mL) Giffard Ginger of the Indies
1½ oz (45 mL) blueberry vodka
1½ oz (45 mL) lemonade
splash of cranberry juice (for colour)

GLASS Large cocktail glass
METHOD In a shaker, muddle basil, lemon,
    and pepper, then add remaining ingredients.
    Shake and double-strain into glass.
GARNISH Lemon twist and basil leaf

el Greco

The Sugar Shack

The Sugar Shack ♈ ♈ ♈
HOME BARTENDER SARAH SHEA

2 oz (60 mL) rye whiskey (Bulleit Rye)
⅔ oz (20 mL) L'Éraporteross apéritif
1 oz (30 mL) Silk Road Spicy Mandarin Syrup
   (p. 183)
½ oz (15 mL) organic mandarin orange juice
2 dashes Bitter Truth Jerry Thomas' Own
   Decanter Bitters

GLASS Large cocktail glass
METHOD Shake ingredients with ice and
   double-strain into glass.
GARNISH Roughly torn mandarin peel spiral

Autumn Ethereal ♈ ♈
GUEST BARTENDER MACKENZIE WHEELER

1½ oz (45 mL) Apple Cinnamon Vodka (p. 173)
½ oz (15 mL) Navan Vanilla Cognac
¼ oz (7.5 mL) Sugar Syrup (p. 183)
2 dashes Fee Brothers' Aztec Chocolate Bitters
1 whole egg

GLASS Wine glass
METHOD Shake ingredients with ice and
   double-strain into glass.
GARNISH Freshly ground nutmeg

Rum Plum Sour ᵞ ᵞ ᵞ
GUEST BARTENDER BRENDAN BREWSTER

1½ oz (45 mL) dark rum (Gosling's Black Seal)
½ oz (15 mL) lemon juice
¾ oz (22.5 mL) Sugar Syrup (p. 183)
1 oz (30 mL) golden plum juice

GLASS Old fashioned / Rocks
METHOD Shake ingredients with ice, then
   double-strain into glass.
GARNISH Dash a line of Angostura Bitters
   across foam

Click Your Heels Thrice ᵞ ᵞ ᵞ
The result of Shawn helping Dean McLeod of
Lighthouse Brewing prepare a hibiscus-infused
cask beer. Shawn made a syrup for Dean to
flavour the beer, then cut the syrup with vodka
and played around with it. A few weeks later, he
reformulated the liqueur and this cocktail was
the outcome.

1½ oz (45 mL) akvavit (Bornholmer)
½ oz (15 mL) bianco vermouth
   (Martini & Rossi Bianco)
½ oz (15 mL) Hibiscus Liqueur (p. 179)
½ oz (15 mL) lemon juice
2 dashes Regans' Orange Bitters

GLASS Large cocktail glass
METHOD Stir ingredients with ice and
   double-strain into glass.
GARNISH Orange twist

Click Your Heels Thrice

Visceral and Violent

Visceral and Violent ᵧ

GUEST BARTENDER JOSH BOUDREAU

8 fresh raspberries
4 large mint leaves
2 oz (60 mL) bourbon whiskey (Buffalo Trace)
¼ oz (7.5 mL) absinthe (Lucid)
½ oz (15 mL) maple syrup

GLASS Tasting glass
METHOD In a shaker tin or Boston glass,
    muddle raspberries and mint. Add remain-
    ing ingredients. Shake with ice and
    double-strain into glass.
GARNISH Lemon twist (use to spritz drink
    and then discard)

Jamaican Sazerac ᵧ ᵧ

A nice variation in a world where there just
aren't enough spirit-forward rum cocktails. The
spicy pimento dram helps engage the senses
when you sip, the same way absinthe does.

2 oz (60 mL) gold rum (Appleton Estate V/X)
⅓ oz (10 mL) Pineapple Syrup (p. 181)
2 dashes House Made Roasted Pineapple
    Bitters
House Made Pimento Dram, to rinse glass

GLASS Old fashioned / Rocks
METHOD Stir rum, Pineapple Syrup, and bit-
    ters with ice and double-strain into House
    Made Pimento Dram–rinsed glass.

Grown Up Roy Rogers ⓨ ⓨ

Inspired by the Southern Cola at Atlanta's Holeman & Finch, this refreshing yet spicy variation on the children's drink of our youth gets better as the ice melts down.

1⅔ oz (50 mL) Amaro Ramazzotti
8 oz (237 mL) bottle Coca-Cola
Cardamom & Pomegranate Ice Cubes (p. 173)

GLASS Old fashioned / Rocks
METHOD Build amaro and cola over Cardamom & Pomegranate Ice Cubes.
GARNISH Fresh mint and pomegranate seeds

Shiso Sour ⓨ ⓨ ⓨ

GUEST BARTENDER BRENDAN BREWSTER

2 oz (60 mL) gin (Hendrick's)
1 oz (30 mL) Giffard Ginger of the Indies
3 or 4 shiso leaves (green perilla or *Perilla frutescens* var. *crispa*), gently muddled
¾ oz (22.5 mL) lime juice
1 dash Sugar Syrup (p. 183)
1 egg white

GLASS Old fashioned / Rocks
METHOD Dry-shake all ingredients with Hawthorne spring (see Bartender's Tip), then wet-shake with ice. Double-strain into glass.
GARNISH Cucumber slice and shiso leaf, floating on the foam

BARTENDER'S TIP Remove spring from your Hawthorne strainer and throw it in the shaker along with the ingredients. As you shake, the spring whisks everything together. Remove spring from shaker before adding ice for wet shake.

Shiso Sour

Normandy Swizzle

Normandy Swizzle ⅄ ⅄

The result of one of our experimental nights showcasing Janice Mansfield's House Made line of bitters and syrups. A simple yet delicious swizzle-style cocktail using her falernum and bitters.

2 oz (60 mL) calvados (Père Magloire)
½ oz (15 mL) House Made Falernum
1 oz (30 mL) lime juice
3 dashes House Made Grapefruit Bitters

GLASS Highball
METHOD Build ingredients in glass over
    crushed ice and swizzle.
GARNISH Lime slice

BC Red Snapper ⅄

The Red Snapper predates the Caesar and uses almost the same ingredients. The oily and smoky potato notes of Schramm vodka along with the crisp refreshing mouth feel of the fresh veggies make this one vodka cocktail Shawn is happy to submit.

4 grape tomatoes
3 slivers red pepper
2 oz (60 mL) potato vodka (Schramm)
2 dashes Tabasco or Worcestershire sauce
⅓ oz (10 mL) lime juice
splash of Mott's Clamato

GLASS Large cocktail glass, rimmed with
    celery salt
METHOD In a shaker, muddle vegetables,
    then add remaining ingredients. Shake with
    ice and double-strain into glass.
GARNISH Freshly cracked pepper

Iced Mayan Mocha ⅄

GUEST BARTENDER RYAN MALCOLM

1 oz (30 mL) pisco (Capel)
½ oz (15 mL) dark crème de cacao
½ oz (15 mL) vanilla liqueur
    (Giffard Vanille de Madagascar)
3 dashes Fee Brothers' Aztec Chocolate Bitters
pinch of chili flakes
2 dashes Tabasco sauce
3 oz (90 mL) milk
2 oz (60 mL) chilled espresso

GLASS Highball / Collins
METHOD Stir all ingredients except espresso
    with ice. Double-strain into glass over ice,
    then layer espresso on top.
GARNISH Flamed orange zest

Tequila North ⅄ ⅄

GUEST BARTENDER VINCENT VANDERHEIDE

1½ oz (45 mL) tequila blanco (el Jimador)
½ oz (15 mL) pear liqueur (Giffard)
½ oz (15 mL) St. Germain Elderflower Liqueur
1 oz (30 mL) Venturi-Schulze Verjus

GLASS Large cocktail glass
METHOD Shake ingredients with ice and
    double-strain into glass.
GARNISH Granny Smith apple slice

Jenkins! ♈

GUEST BARTENDER KATIE MCDONALD

2 oz (60 mL) Hendrick's Gin
¾ oz (22.5 mL) lemon juice
¾ oz (22.5 mL) lychee liqueur
    (Giffard Lichi-Li)
½ oz (15 mL) Honey Syrup (p. 179)
¼ oz (7.5 mL) rosewater

GLASS Large cocktail glass
METHOD Shake ingredients with ice and
    double-strain into glass.
GARNISH Dried rose petals

Grim Rose ↡

After discovering The Rose in Ted Haigh's
book *Vintage Spirits and Forgotten
Cocktails*, Nate fell in love with the idea of
vermouth/quinquina–based cocktails. This
is his idea of dessert and digestif in one
delicious treat.

2 oz (60 mL) Dubonnet Rouge
⅔ oz (20 mL) Fernet-Branca
¼ oz (7.5 mL) grenadine

GLASS Ornate port glass
METHOD Shake ingredients with ice and
    double-strain into glass.
GARNISH Picked cherry

Sicilian Smash ᵧ

Shawn likes to think that if young Vito Corleone had a drink in his hand in the Old Country, this one would be pretty close to it. A little bit Mai Tai, a little bit Caipirinha, and a lot Italian.

8 mint leaves
half a lemon
1 oz (30 mL) Amaro Averna
1 oz (30 mL) Fernet-Branca
½ oz (15 mL) orgeat syrup (Giffard)

GLASS Old fashioned / Rocks
METHOD In a Boston glass, muddle mint and lemon, then add remaining ingredients. Shake with ice and strain into glass over crushed ice.
GARNISH Lemon wedge and mint sprig

The Clover Point ᵧ ᵧ

HOME BARTENDER DAVE KELSEY

2 tsp (10 mL) fresh pomegranate seeds
1 oz (30 mL) tequila blanco
1 oz (30 mL) Aperol
¼ oz (7.5 mL) lime juice

GLASS Small wine glass
METHOD In the bottom part of a Boston shaker, muddle pomegranate seeds, then add remaining ingredients. Shake with ice and double-strain into glass.

Moscow Monk ᵧ ᵧ

GUEST BARTENDER RYAN MALCOLM

½ oz (15 mL) Green Chartreuse
2 sprigs fresh thyme
1½ oz (45 mL) vodka (Russian Standard)
½ oz (15 mL) Ginger Syrup (p. 178)
½ oz (15 mL) lime juice
ginger beer, to top

GLASS Highball / Collins
METHOD In glass, pour Chartreuse over
    thyme sprigs and light on fire. Shake vodka,
    syrup, and lime juice with ice and single-
    strain over lit thyme to extinguish. Top up
    with ginger beer.
GARNISH Charred thyme sprig

High Tea in Milan ᵧ

An awesome alternative to the modern mon-
strosities that come via plastic-bottle pre-mixes
where you just add cola (off a gun). A nice
afternoon treat for the amaro fans out there.

1 oz (30 mL) Amaro Ramazzotti
1 oz (30 mL) Amaro Lucano
1 oz (30 mL) Cynar
1 oz (30 mL) lemon juice
Fentimans Tonic Water, to top

GLASS Vintage teapot and teacup
METHOD In a teapot, build Amaro
    Ramazzotti, Amaro Lucano, Cynar, and
    lemon juice over ice. Top up with tonic.
GARNISH Lemon slice

High Tea in Milan

Rosemary's Baby

Rosemary's Baby ♆ ♆

GUEST BARTENDER SIMON OGDEN

1 fresh rosemary sprig
½ oz (15 mL) Green Chartreuse
1 oz (30 mL) London dry gin
1 oz (30 mL) Galliano
1 oz (30 mL) lemon juice

GLASS Large cocktail glass
METHOD In glass, add rosemary sprig and
    Chartreuse; set alight. Shake remaining
    ingredients with ice and pour into glass to
    douse. Stir to combine and then discard
    rosemary sprig.

Chivalrous Breakfast ♆

Breaking the seal has never been so reward-
ing. Don't be shy about using jam in cocktails.
Salvatore Calabrese's legendary Breakfast
Martini was essentially a White Lady until he
raided his pantry one fine morning.

1½ oz (45 mL) blended Scotch whisky
    (Chivas Regal)
½ oz (15 mL) Giffard Ginger of the Indies
½ oz (15 mL) apricot liqueur
    (Giffard Abricot du Roussillon)
2 barspoons marmalade
1 oz (30 mL) orange juice

GLASS Mason jar
METHOD Shake all ingredients with ice and
    dirty-strain into jar.
GARNISH Ginger disc and orange wedge

Kamikaze Carrot ♈ ♈

GUEST BARTENDER VINCENT VANDERHEIDE

1 oz (30 mL) Ginger Infused Gin (p. 177)
1 oz (30 mL) triple sec (Cointreau)
½ oz (15 mL) Giffard Ginger of the Indies
1 oz (30 mL) carrot juice
3 drops Angostura Orange Bitters
soda, to top

GLASS Highball / Collins
METHOD Shake first 5 ingredients with ice
    and double-strain into ice-filled glass. Top
    with soda.
GARNISH Cracked pepper and lemon slices

T. Roosevelt ♈

HOME BARTENDER BRUCE GILLESPIE

¾ oz (22.5 mL) dark rum (Gosling's Black Seal)
¾ oz (22.5 mL) Tennessee whiskey
    (Gentleman Jack)
½ oz (15 mL) cachaça (Sagatiba Pura)
½ oz (15 mL) lime juice
agave syrup, to balance/sweeten the citrus

GLASS Large cocktail glass
METHOD Shake ingredients with ice and
    double-strain into glass.
GARNISH Maraschino cherry

T. Roosevelt

Reverse Cosmosis

Reverse Cosmosis ▼ ▼

Think of this as a Cosmopolitan for people who don't like Cosmopolitans. The same drink but deconstructed and reassembled with some quality ingredients.

2 lime zests
1½ oz (45 mL) London dry gin (Beefeater 24)
¾ oz (22.5 mL) triple sec (Cointreau)
½ oz (15 mL) Cranberry Syrup (p. 176)
2 dashes Peychaud's Bitters

GLASS Small cocktail glass
METHOD Place lime zests in mixing glass or tin. Add remaining ingredients, stir with ice, and double-strain into glass.
GARNISH Flamed orange zest

Peko Bou ▼ ▼

Everyone needs a tea cocktail. They are a lot like melon ballers—many people have them kicking around, even though they rarely use them. An easy recipe that perks up a standard Boulevardier.

1½ oz (45 mL) Pekoe Infused Bourbon (p. 181)
¾ oz (22.5 mL) Cynar
¾ oz (22.5 mL) sweet vermouth (Cinzano Rosso)

GLASS Small cocktail glass
METHOD Stir ingredients with ice and strain into glass.
GARNISH Orange zest

The Lulu ℥

HOME BARTENDER DAVE KELSEY

¾ oz (22.5 mL) pisco (Capel)
¾ oz (22.5 mL) St. Germain Elderflower
    Liqueur
¾ oz (22.5 mL) Rosemary Syrup (p. 182)
½ oz (15 mL) lime juice

GLASS Large cocktail glass
METHOD Shake all ingredients with ice and
    double-strain into glass.

Before It Was Cool ℥ ℥

This is a bit of a satire of the hipster culture
that is prevalent in almost any city these days.
Hipsters love bourbon, bitters, and coffee, and
most definitely before it was cool.

2 oz (60 mL) bourbon whiskey
    (Bulleit Bourbon)
1 oz (30 mL) Espresso Syrup (p. 177)
    (see Bartender's Tip)
1½ oz (45 mL) half-and-half
1 barspoon Angostura Aromatic Bitters

GLASS Small old fashioned / Rocks
METHOD Shake ingredients with ice and
    double-strain neat.
GARNISH Cinnamon stencilled moustache or
    plain cinnamon sprinkle

BARTENDER'S TIP The espresso syrup
    called for in this recipe should ideally be
    made with Discovery Coffee beans. This will
    help create the specific flavour profile we
    want to achieve in this cocktail.

Before It Was Cool

Canes & Coatails

Canes & Coatails Ɏ Ɏ

This is Nate's interpretation of the concept, marketing, and culture surrounding the Hendrick's Gin brand. We've been to many events held by them, and they showcase their product in a very *Alice in Wonderland* / Victorian way. Hendrick's Gin is distilled with rose petals and cucumber.

1-inch (2.5 cm) piece fresh cucumber
1½ oz (45 mL) Hendrick's Gin
1 oz (30 mL) rose wine (Marqués de Cáceres)
⅔ oz (20 mL) Rhubarb Syrup (p. 182)
scant dash celery bitters (Bitter Truth)

GLASS Large cocktail glass
METHOD In a shaker tin, muddle cucumber, add remaining ingredients, and shake. Double strain into glass.
GARNISH Cucumber slice on the rim of the glass

Sherry Bobbins Ɏ Ɏ

Every menu should include a sherry cocktail of some sort. This is a balanced Oloroso Sherry cocktail in the vein of classic English-style drinks. Aptly named after a parodied *Simpsons* character.

1⅓ oz (40 mL) Pimm's No. 1 Cup
⅔ oz (20 mL) Oloroso Sherry
    (Lustau East India Solera)
⅔ oz (20 mL) grapefruit juice
1 barspoon Earl Grey Tea Syrup (p. 176)
1 dash grapefruit bitters (Bitter Truth)

GLASS Large cocktail glass
METHOD Shake ingredients with ice and double-strain into glass.
GARNISH Grapefruit twist

Old Thyme Prairie Berry Fizz ♈ ♈ ♈

Nate's entry into the 2011 Art of the Cocktail competition, which had the theme of "Farmer's Market." This cocktail spawned the Saskatoon Liqueur (p. 182), which in turn led to the creation of many other cocktails.

1½ oz (45 mL) London dry gin (Tanqueray)
1 oz (30 mL) Saskatoon Liqueur (p. 182)
3 dashes lavender bitters (House Made)
1 oz (30 mL) lemon juice
Thyme Soda (p. 183), to top

GLASS Fizz glass
METHOD Shake gin, liqueur, bitters, and
    juice with ice and double-strain into glass.
    Top up with Thyme Soda.
GARNISH Thyme sprig

Koala Mojito ♈ ♈

A classic mojito but with the introduction of eucalyptus oil into the ice.

1⅔ oz (50 mL) white rum (Havana Club 3 Year)
½ oz (15 mL) Sugar Syrup (p. 183)
1 oz (30 mL) soda water
Lime & Eucalyptus Crushed Ice (p. 180)

GLASS Highball glass
METHOD Swizzle rum, syrup, and soda water
    with Lime & Eucalyptus Crushed Ice.
GARNISH Mint sprig

Koala Mojito

Hemming Gucci

Hemming Gucci ♟ ♟ ♟

GUEST BARTENDER JJ SKIDMORE

1 oz (30 mL) tequila blanco
½ oz (15 mL) Housemade Limoncello (p. 180)
1 oz (30 mL) lime juice
1 oz (30 mL) ruby red grapefruit juice
3 dashes Bitter Truth Lemon Bitters
½ oz (15 mL) Campari

GLASS Highball / Collins, half-rimmed with
    sea salt
METHOD Build tequila, limoncello, juices,
    and bitters in glass over ice, then float
    Campari.
GARNISH Long grapefruit twist

Mr. Anderson ♟

Named after one of Shawn's best mates and the
best man at his wedding. He loved his sweeter-
style cocktails, and this filled the bill perfectly.
He thought it was a hell of a compliment to have
this on the menu for many months and was dev-
astated when it got cut.

1½ oz (45 mL) Irish whiskey (Jameson)
1 oz (30 mL) amaretto (Disaronno)
1 barspoon fig jam
1 oz (30 mL) lime juice

GLASS Large cocktail glass
METHOD Shake ingredients with ice and
    double-strain into glass.
GARNISH Lime slice on the rim of the glass

Blume Sauer ⅄

The literal German translation is "flower sour." Essentially an ode to the Trinidad Sour, which dared to use a whole ounce of Angostura Bitters. Orgeat syrup is a fantastic option for taming intense flavours at either end of the bitter/floral spectrum.

1 oz (30 mL) cachaça (Leblon)
1 oz (30 mL) violet liqueur (Bitter Truth)
½ oz (15 mL) orgeat syrup (Giffard)
1 oz (30 mL) lemon juice
1 egg white

GLASS Fizz glass
METHOD Hard-shake ingredients with ice and
    double-strain into glass.

Invierno de Jerez ⅄ ⅄ ⅄

GUEST BARTENDER VINCENT VANDERHEIDE

1 oz (30 mL) butternut squash juice
1 oz (30 mL) solera sherry
    (Lustau East India Solera)
1 oz (30 mL) pear liqueur (Giffard)
⅓ oz (10 mL) Navan Vanilla Cognac Liqueur
1 dash Fee Brothers' West Indian Orange Bitters
3 dashes Jerez sherry vinegar

GLASS Large cocktail glass
METHOD Shake all ingredients with ice and
    double-strain into glass.
GARNISH Spanked sage sprig

Invierno de Jerez

Sandy Blonde

Sandy Blonde ☉

This very approachable and easy-going cocktail
has been on our list for years.

1 oz (30 mL) Zubrowka Bison Grass Vodka
1 oz (30 mL) calvados
½ oz (15 mL) elderflower cordial
1 dash peach bitters (Fee Brothers)
1 oz (30 mL) lime juice

GLASS Large cocktail glass
METHOD Shake ingredients with ice and
    double-strain into glass.
GARNISH Lime slice on the rim of the glass

PDX ☉ ☉ ☉

HOME BARTENDER SARAH SHEA

1½ oz (45 mL) New Western dry gin (Aviation)
½ oz (15 mL) Yellow Chartreuse
½ oz (15 mL) Sugar Syrup (p. 183)
¼ oz (7.5 mL) Pok Pok Som drinking vinegar
¼ oz (7.5 mL) Benedictine

GLASS Large cocktail glass
METHOD In a mixing glass, stir ingredients
    with ice and double-strain into glass.

Crouching Tiger Y Y

GUEST BARTENDER DIRK VANDERWAL

4-inch (10 cm) piece fresh cucumber, sliced
    and quartered
1 oz (30 mL) London dry gin
    (Tanqueray No. Ten)
1 oz (30 mL) Giffard Ginger of the Indies
1½ oz (45 mL) Ginger Syrup (p. 178)
juice from 1 lime

GLASS Old fashioned / Rocks
METHOD In a shaker, muddle cucumber, then
    add remaining ingredients and shake with
    ice. Double-strain into glass over fresh ice.
GARNISH Cucumber slices and lime slice

Crouching Tiger

Flips

Every year we release our cold winter menu, which features the addition of a flips section. Flips were originally a joke, inserted to see if people would go for a cocktail with a whole egg in it. After our first winter, we realized that people do like this classic cocktail, which is basically alcoholic custard. And we soon discovered that everything tastes better in a flip.

Childhood Flip (left)
and Krak Nog (right)

Childhood Flip Y

Named for the apple custard turnovers Shawn used to get from the local bakery on his way to school. The combination of custard, apples, and pastry was addictive then, and now it's available in liquid form.

1 oz (30 mL) Irish whiskey (Bushmills)
½ oz (15 mL) Frangelico
½ oz (15 mL) Apfelkorn apple schnapps
½ oz (15 mL) lemon juice
½ oz (15 mL) Sugar Syrup (p. 183)
1 whole egg

GLASS Flip glass
METHOD Hard-shake all ingredients with ice and double-strain into glass.
GARNISH Freshly ground nutmeg

Flip the Switch Y Y Y

Switchel is usually enjoyed in the hotter months, but if you still have some kicking around, here's a drink that will go down far too easy in the colder months.

1½ oz (45 mL) Canadian whisky
    (Forty Creek Barrel Select)
1½ oz (45 mL) Switchel (p. 183)
½ oz (15 mL) apricot liqueur
    (Giffard Abricot du Roussillon)
1 whole egg

GLASS Flip glass
METHOD Hard-shake ingredients with ice and double-strain into glass.
GARNISH Dried apricot and ground nutmeg

Honolulu Ink Flip ♈ ♈

Designed to be an entry-level flip for those who don't want to hit the absinthe or sherry just yet. Very approachable ingredients help introduce this niche corner of classic mixology to people who are in the market for a tasty winter rum drink.

2 oz (60 mL) spiced rum (Sailor Jerry)
½ oz (15 mL) vanilla liqueur
    (Giffard Vanille de Madagascar)
2 dashes Orange Cinnamon Tincture (p. 181)
1 whole egg

GLASS Flip glass
METHOD Hard-shake ingredients with ice and
    double-strain into glass.
GARNISH Freshly ground nutmeg

Fernadito Flip ♈ ♈

The epitome of the "everything is better in a flip" mantra. Most people shy away from Fernet-Branca, but when mixed with dairy or eggs, it becomes smooth and its mint flavours come forward.

2 oz (60 mL) Fernet-Branca
½ oz (15 mL) Cola Syrup (p. 176)
1 whole egg

GLASS Flip glass
METHOD Hard-shake ingredients with ice and
    double-strain into glass.
GARNISH Freshly ground nutmeg

New World Meets Old World Flip ⅄

HOME BARTENDER JANICE MANSFIELD

1½ oz (45 mL) reposado tequila
¾ oz (22.5 mL) Yellow Chartreuse
½ oz (15 mL) Sugar Syrup (p. 183)
1 whole egg
2 to 3 dashes Bitter Truth Jerry Thomas' Own
   Decanter Bitters

GLASS Large cocktail glass
METHOD Dry-shake all ingredients, then wet-
   shake with ice. Double-strain into glass.
GARNISH Freshly ground nutmeg

Absinthe Flip ⅄

Another flip that showcases how well even the
hardest spirits can be moulded into smooth,
creamy cocktails with the introduction of an egg.

2 oz (60 mL) absinthe (Taboo)
⅔ oz (20 mL) elderflower cordial (Bottlegreen)
1 whole egg

GLASS Flip glass
METHOD Hard-shake ingredients with ice and
   double-strain into glass.
GARNISH Freshly ground nutmeg

Krak Nog ⅋

Easily the most fun Nate has making eggnog from scratch. The robust and spicy backbone of Kraken rum lends beautifully to the finished texture of the drink.

2 oz (60 mL) Kraken Black Spiced Rum
2 heaping barspoons powdered sugar
2 dashes ground nutmeg
2 dashes ground cinnamon
2 oz (60 mL) half-and-half
1 whole egg
half a vanilla bean

GLASS Nog glass
METHOD Hard-shake all ingredients with ice and double-strain into glass.
GARNISH Freshly ground nutmeg and cinnamon stick

Burning Bridges ⅋ ⅋ ⅋

Saskatoon is called the city of bridges in Canada. Using Saskatoon Liqueur (p. 182) as well as smoky, earthy mezcal makes this the Burning Bridges Flip.

2 oz (60 mL) Saskatoon Liqueur (p. 182)
½ oz (15 mL) Sugar Syrup (p. 183)
1 barspoon mezcal (Del Maguey Vida)
2 dashes chocolate bitters (Bitter Truth)

GLASS Flip glass
METHOD Shake ingredients with ice and double-strain into glass.

Burning Bridges

Beer/Cider Cocktails

Beer cocktails have become a mainstay trend in most
bars and cocktail menus the world over. There is
always some contention between cocktail bartenders and artisanal brewmasters—some say beer is a
great base to build cocktails off, while the brewers
argue they don't want their brews played with. On the
other hand, cideries love to have their products used
in cocktails, so there's another opinion. Whichever
camp you align with, these cocktails are tasty.

Gaarden Hoe

Gaarden Hoe 🍸

GUEST BARTENDER BROOKE LEVIE

¾ oz (22.5 mL) London dry gin (Beefeater)
¾ oz (22.5 mL) bianco vermouth (Martini Bianco)
¾ oz (22.5 mL) Bottlegreen Elderflower Cordial
¾ oz (22.5 mL) lemon juice
2 dashes lemon bitters (Bitter Truth)
Hoegaarden beer, to top

GLASS Wine glass
METHOD Shake all ingredients except Hoegaarden with ice. Double-strain into glass and top up with beer.
GARNISH Lemon twist

The Tsar 🍸🍸

GUEST BARTENDER KEN GIFFORD

2 oz (60 mL) overproof bourbon whiskey (Booker's Bourbon)
¾ oz (22.5 mL) Driftwood Singularity Reduction (p. 176)
¾ oz (22.5 mL) Aperol
3 or 4 dashes orange bitters

GLASS Old fashioned / Rocks
METHOD In a mixing glass, stir all ingredients together. Strain into chilled glass.
GARNISH Flamed orange peel spiral

Kentucky P'ale ♈ ♈

GUEST BARTENDER KEN GIFFORD

2 oz (60 mL) bourbon whiskey
    (Woodford Reserve)
½ oz (15 mL) apricot liqueur
    (Giffard Abricot du Roussillon)
⅓ oz (10 mL) Phillips Amnesiac IPA
    Reduction (p. 181)
1 tsp (5 mL) Honey Syrup (p. 179)
2 dashes Angostura Bitters

GLASS Old fashioned / Rocks
METHOD In a mixing glass, stir all ingredi-
    ents together. Strain into chilled glass.
GARNISH Lemon slice (twist over drink then
    discard) and flamed orange peel spiral (add
    to glass)

Tuesday ♈

GUEST BARTENDER SAMANTHA CASUGA

2 oz (60 mL) silver tequila
½ oz (15 mL) agave syrup
½ oz (15 mL) lime juice
2 thin slices fresh jalapeno pepper
handful cilantro
1 oz (30 mL) Corona

GLASS Old fashioned / Rocks
METHOD Shake tequila, agave, lime, jalapeno,
    and cilantro with ice. Strain into glass over
    fresh ice and top with Corona float.
GARNISH Cilantro sprig

The Beverage Formerly Known as Glo Refresh ♈ ♈

GUEST BARTENDER RYAN MALCOLM

1 sprig Thai basil
1 oz (30 mL) spiced rum (Sailor Jerry)
½ oz (15 mL) Benedictine
½ oz (15 mL) Giffard Ginger of the Indies
½ oz (15 mL) lemon juice
¼ oz (7.5 mL) Lemongrass Syrup (p. 180)
dry cider, to top

GLASS Old fashioned / Rocks
METHOD In a shaker, muddle basil. Add
    rum, liqueurs, lemon juice, and syrup.
    Shake with ice. Single-strain into glass,
    then top with dry cider.
GARNISH Lemongrass stalk

Five Magics ♈ ♈
GUEST BARTENDER MACKENZIE WHEELER

2 oz (60 mL) white rum
    (Banks 5 Island Rum)
1/2 oz (15 mL) St. Germain Elderflower
    Liqueur
3/4 oz (22.5 mL) lemon juice
3 dashes peach bitters (Fee Brothers)
1/4 oz (7.5 mL) Sugar Syrup (p. 183)
3/4 oz (22.5 mL) Früli strawberry beer

GLASS Large cocktail glass
METHOD Shake all ingredients except
    beer with ice, then double-strain into
    glass. Add beer and stir gently to
    incorporate.
GARNISH Grapefruit zest

Pop the Strawberry ᵧ ᵧ

The product of one of our many beer cocktail nights: a sweet and floral cocktail that really showcases not only the G'Vine gin but also the Früli strawberry beer.

1½ oz (45 mL) G'Vine Floraison Gin
½ oz (15 mL) Rhubarb Syrup (p. 182)
½ oz (15 mL) lime juice
1 oz (30 mL) Früli strawberry beer

GLASS Large cocktail glass
METHOD Shake ingredients with ice and
    double-strain into glass.

Pop Top Collins ᵧ ᵧ ᵧ

This Collins replaces soda with the iconic "pop top" beer: Grolsch. The pisco and Saskatoon Liqueur (p. 182) help punch up the base and give the lager something to latch on to. The result is a very refreshing beer cocktail.

1½ oz (45 mL) pisco (Capel)
½ oz (15 mL) Saskatoon Liqueur (p. 182)
½ oz (15 mL) Sugar Syrup (p. 183)
2 dashes House Made Cherry Bitters
¾ oz (22.5 mL) lemon juice
lager (Grolsch), to top

GLASS Highball
METHOD In glass, build pisco, liqueur,
    syrup, bitters, and lemon juice over ice.
    Top with lager.
GARNISH Lemon slice and cherry

the Bartenders

Here on the island, we are a tight-knit group. Over the next few pages, you'll be introduced to some of the incredibly talented and passionate bartenders we are proud to call friends. You'll also meet some wonderful home bartenders who are a part of our community. Come and visit us around town—we'd love to share our passion for cocktails with you in person!

J. Adam Bonneau

Adam's interest in making fine cocktails comes from his love of people. He truly believes that great food coupled with unbelievable drinks can set the mood for an amazing night. His quest for the perfect cocktail took him across Canada, before he landed here in Victoria. Along the way, he had some great teachers who helped him develop a style to call his own. Simple, concise, and to the point are the principles that make up the foundation of his style. Just the right amount of one ingredient balanced harmoniously with another, without all the bells and whistles, is the middle ground where he likes to tend bar. Twelve years of experience in the business have led him to this philosophy: "I would like you to enjoy my cocktail, I would like you to enjoy my bar, but most of all I would like you to enjoy yourself."

Josh Boudreau

Josh has been a professional bartender for the past three years. He balances his passion for customer service and cocktail creation with a love of music, fronting two popular Victoria rock bands on lead guitar. Josh was awarded the title of "Best Bartender in the Pacific Northwest" at the 2011 Art of the Cocktail competition for professionals.

Brendan Brewster

Brendan began his career in the hospitality industry peeling potatoes in an Irish pub in the Netherlands and quickly fell in love with the characters, accents, stresses, and successes. And, of course, the pretty, pretty bottles. Time behind the stick in Ireland taught him about black gold, a little more about accents, and yet more about pretty bottles. An extended tour in Vancouver saw Brendan working as a bar manager, promoter, doorman, and head barkeep everywhere from gritty basement punk-rock bars to neighbourhood pubs, stadium-adjacent sports bars, and boutique restaurants. Bitten hard by the classic cocktail bug a few years back, Brendan staged with some of Vancouver's pre-eminent bartenders and continues to take every opportunity to better learn his craft. He recently relocated to Vancouver Island to teach bartending and is the co-founder of Stay Busy Bar Service. Obsessed with flavour affinities, cocktails, the history of alcohol, and bartending as a trade, Brendan believes that the culture of food and drink helps to provide connection to both others and history itself through a shared morsel or dram.

Samantha Casuga

Samantha is a true lover of the finer things in life. Having worked various positions in the industry, it was her fervour for great food and drink that carried her into the bartending world. Beginning her journey in Calgary, Alberta, Samantha quickly climbed her way up, gaining knowledge and experience that helped evolve her skills. Since moving to Victoria, she has worked closely with peers and mentors at places like Veneto Tapa Lounge, Vis à Vis Wine & Charcuterie Bar, and The Black Hat by Bistro28, and she finds immense encouragement from those around her. Being around chefs, bartenders, sommeliers, and other connoisseurs of the food and beverage realm, Samantha is continually inspired and challenged, which she loves. A big-city girl at heart, she indulges in what the island offers her in terms of ingredients, flavours, and muses. Working her way up to becoming a certified sommelier, Samantha hopes to one day work hands-on with her favourite libation: wine.

Until then she will continue to expand her repertoire, encourage customers to push the boundaries of their palates, and share what she finds joyful to the taste buds—and always with a smile and a laugh.

Ken Gifford

Ken has an affinity for bold whiskies, delicate gins, and all things bitter. Having tended bars in Australia and on St. Martin and Vancouver Island, he embraces the roaming lifestyle the bar allows and the creativity it fosters. Ken's presence behind the bar can be described as energetic, creative, and approachable. He has a passion and respect for classic cocktails and their artful creation. He is interested in all spirits as well as the distillation process. He also knows that slinging drinks is only a small part of a barkeep's job, and that is what keeps it interesting. Ken considers himself a young bartender eager to learn and progress his palate.

Emily Henderson

While Emily also wears the hat of general manager, she is most at home behind the bar. But bartending was something that happened to her somewhat by accident. She started doing it as a means to travel and go to school, but just when she started to think about leaving it, she realized there was way more about bartending that she would miss than she would be happy to part with. An eighteen-month stint working in a bar in Australia in the early 2000s showed her how much was going on in bartending in other parts of the world and how much more there was to learn. Inspired, she returned to Victoria and has been bartending ever since. She loves to "finger paint" with spirits, interact with and take care of the random cross-section of people she gets to serve, and embrace the hustle of a busy bar. She also loves to host a good party.

Brooke Levie

When Brooke arrives at a party, it's generally with a punch bowl full of mysterious ingredients no one recognizes but that is always the first bowl to run dry. With fifteen years experience in Italian, French, and Caribbean restaurants, he's become cultured in fine wines, beers, and a wide range of cocktails. "I've come a long way from keg parties with my buddies on Galiano Island," he says. "Though with the draft beer available these days, I could throw one hell of a party!"

Brooke's original dream of becoming a chef morphed into a passion for cocktail culture. After joining the Marina Restaurant as bar manager, Brooke's zeal was lifted to another level. With this thirst for knowledge, he introduced himself to Shawn Soole at Clive's Classic Lounge. After countless tastings, seminars, and far too many bottles of bitters, he reinvented the Marina's beverage program and is now stoked to get paid for doing what he loves.

Ryan Malcolm

Ryan was born and raised in Victoria. After being inspired by his older brother (also a bartender), he went out and bought his first bar book when he was just fifteen. Led by a passion for the food and beverage industry, Ryan found himself working as a barista after high school, biding his time until he attained the legal age to serve alcohol. At the age of nineteen, Ryan took his first job at a restaurant as a bar back. By twenty, he had become the bar manager. His mantra is "craft cocktails for everyday people." He enjoys using Old World ingredients, such as Chartreuse and Benedictine, and giving them a New World spin that makes them approachable for everyone. Ryan is also the rep for New Theatre Spirits & Tonics, a Victoria-based company that makes original-style tonic.

Katie McDonald

Dashing her family's hopes that she would become a studious, professional woman, Katie began her career mixing drinks after attending university. Behind the bar, she inspires passion in patrons and fellow bartenders alike. Katie has created numerous items based on the theory "if you can't find the ingredient you want, make it." She experiments and creates in the name of good taste and good experience with a patron-centred approach. The people she serves and those in her work community inspire her creativity and unique style. She has helped out with Victoria's cocktail festival, Art of the Cocktail, since its creation, co-hosted a radio segment, and recently bartended at Tales of the Cocktail in Vancouver.

Simon Ogden

For the past twenty-two years, Simon has
been a professional bartender and mentor
all over British Columbia. He has developed his discipline and technique with
experience in every facet of the bar industry, from neighbourhood watering holes to
high-volume Granville Street nightclubs
to craft cocktail lounges. Simon has been
recognized by Tourism BC as one of the
province's leading service bartenders.
He currently practises and teaches his
philosophy of personalized service and
classic cocktail construction in Victoria,
BC. He is also vice-president, and one of
the founding members, of the Canadian
Professional Bartenders Association.

Stephen Quigley

Stephen was born and raised in Dublin and fell into the industry as an apprentice cook. He subsequently gained experience in all facets of the food industry: from Chinese to Mexican, fine dining to industrial catering. He has criss-crossed the globe, including stints in Ireland, Australia, Scotland, France, and, currently, British Columbia. Stephen began tending bar in Paris in 2000 and decided there and then to permanently trade in his chef's jacket for a waistcoat. He moved to Victoria in 2007 and can now be found behind the bar at Stage Wine Bar in Fernwood.

Cyle Serra

Growing up on Salt Spring Island, Cyle was always close to nature, so it's only natural that he likes his drinks herbaceous and containing ingredients from the earth. Recently he has been studying herbalism to understand what all of the roots and herbs we imbibe actually do to us. He believes that understanding the constituents and effects of herbs can make us all better tenders in the bar. If we can identify a customer's problem—say they are hungover—we can concoct for them a corpse reviver. And if we add herbs like borage or self-heal, which contain, respectively, adrenal gland and liver restorative properties, then we can truly awaken the "dead."

Solomon Siegel

Solomon was born and raised in Victoria and has been working in restaurants since he could hold a coffee pot. Solomon first got behind the bar at his father and uncle's famous restaurant, Pagliacci's. There he developed a natural interest in all things beverage. He opened Victoria's first cocktail bar, Solomon's, in 2008. Shortly after Solomon's closed, he began to teach at various venues around town. He appears regularly on *Island 30*'s "Mixology 101" on CHEK and is a frequent contributor to *EAT Magazine*. He also competed in the finals of the 2011 G'Vine Gin Connoisseur Program in Cognac, France, which is one of the most gruelling cocktail competitions in the world.

JJ Skidmore

It all started in 1988, when JJ got his first job at a deli as a server, sandwich maker, and dishwasher. Since then he has had many jobs, all of them tied to the hospitality industry. While living in Vancouver, he decided to go to bartending school. That was during the nineties, when everything was built around speed, not quality. He landed his first bar job in downtown Vancouver at a pub-style restaurant, where he had to serve many businesspeople, which gave him the chance to really work on his bartending skills. He moved to Vancouver Island when he was transferred here as a part-time paramedic. To supplement his income, he worked at the Longwood Brew Pub in Nanaimo. After moving to Victoria, JJ increased his beer knowledge at Canoe Brewpub. He then became the bar manager at Milestones. This proved to be his biggest bar challenge because he had be everything a bartender is supposed to be: fast, funny, organized, knowledgeable, accommodating, and countless other things. He was then offered a job at Café Brio, one of Victoria's top restaurants, and has taken everything he has learned and tried to make it a true bar experience for his guests. In this industry, you need to make sure you are always learning, and that is what JJ tries to do every day.

Vincent Vanderheide

Vincent moved to Victoria in 2003 to pursue a degree in English literature at the University of Victoria and has been tending bar ever since. Vincent multitasks well, serving fine beers while at the same time creating interesting options for his more cocktail-minded guests. This creates a unique and challenging work environment that is rich in benefits. His home bar functions as a laboratory, black hole, and social space. When Vincent is not at work, he is generally busy "researching."

Dirk VanderWal

Dirk has spent most of his working life in the hospitality industry, but he considers bartending the best job he's ever had. He loves what he does and it shows. Several years after starting at the Delta Victoria Ocean Pointe Resort & Spa, Dirk was offered the chance to join the opening team at LURE Restaurant & Lounge. As the restaurant established itself, he began focusing his attention on the lounge and soon took over the top spot behind the bar. He spent a few years experimenting, educating himself, and honing his craft, then began participating in competitive events. In late 2010, Dirk was crowned "Best Bartender in the Pacific Northwest" by *EAT Magazine*'s panel of judges at Victoria's annual Art of the Cocktail festival. Since then he has been busy continuing to bring classic and contemporary craft cocktails to the crowd at LURE and trying to look like he knows what he is doing.

Mackenzie Wheeler

Mackenzie's first experience with a cocktail was shortly after his nineteenth birthday. It was March 2010, and he was having dinner at a chain restaurant when he took a look at their "martini" list. As reluctant as he is to admit that his first cocktail was concocted of vodka, apple liqueur, melon liqueur, pineapple juice, and lemon juice, it was that drink that began his interest in cocktails and spirits. During the months that followed this first libation, Mackenzie began expanding his home bar with various types of booze and bartending books. However, it wasn't until September 2010 that he finally discovered what bartenders refer to as "craft cocktails." This discovery was due entirely to Art of the Cocktail, the turning point that made Mackenzie see cocktails from a different perspective. In February 2011, he started writing a cocktail blog (thespiritofimbibing. blogspot.com) to help express his passion for drinks and improve his writing skills. Since his first post blog, he has become borderline

OCD over cocktails and spirits. Attending every festival and seminar possible, he is always striving to broaden his knowledge of all things alcoholic.

HOME BARTENDERS

Left to right: Sarah Shea,
Dave Kelsey, Janice Mansfield,
and Bruce Gillespie

Bruce Gillespie

Bruce traces his fascination with cocktails back to the summer of 1975, when he worked at Mulvaney's Restaurant on Granville Island in Vancouver (now The Sandbar). During his time there, he learned a great deal of technique from head bartenders Ron and José and was saved from the monotony of rye and ginger, and rum and cola, pervading university parties. After discovering concoctions such as the Ramos Fizz and the Pousse-Café, he raced out and bought his first Boston shaker and Hawthorne strainer (tools he still uses today).

Since then, in his travels, he has had the good fortune to meet other cocktail enthusiasts and experts and learn many new and traditional mixes of spirits. He learned the "perfect" margarita recipe from Felix, an evening bartender at the Playa de Oro Hotel's Palapa Bar in Mexico. He has engaged in deep conversations about technique and ingredients with Vladislav at the American Bar in the newly renovated Savoy Hotel in London. And he has learned from such characters as Philip Duff, Murray Stenson, and Shawn Soole, among others—all of whom have generously shared their wisdom and good cheer from across the bar.

When he returned to Victoria six years ago after a thirty-four-year absence, Bruce was delighted to find new sources of both thought and supply in friends and fellow home bartenders as well as in the many talented local bartenders. Long live creative mixology!

Dave Kelsey

Dave was invited to accompany a friend to the industry tasting at the first Art of the Cocktail in 2009. There he tasted four drinks: a Bourbon Sour, a Dark and Stormy, something called an iBull (by Solomon Siegel), and a Chartreuse on Ice. Up until that point, Dave's acquaintance with cocktails had been limited to, alas, the gin and tonic and the classic martini. That first Art of the Cocktail serendipitously started a new passion: cocktails. For Dave, a cocktail must look good, be prepared with care, use the best ingredients, and, above all, taste good!

Shawn Soole made Dave his first Negroni, and through Shawn and Nate, Dave has learned a lot.

Janice Mansfield

Janice is the personal chef behind Real Food Made Easy, which provides catering services, meal planning, and meal preparation for people with restricted diets. She also enjoys classic cocktails and incorporates them into catered dinners and special events. In 2009, Janice began experimenting with bitters and creating products she was unable to find in Canada. She soon found demand from others experiencing the same frustration. Those first bitters experiments evolved into House Made Bitters, a line of micro-batch artisanal bitters, with a distinct culinary edge. House Made now produces eight standard flavours of bitters, with a changing selection of one-time, seasonal flavours, as well as a line of cocktail syrups.

Sarah Shea

Sarah's obsession with cocktails took hold after she attended Victoria's first Art of the Cocktail (AOC) in 2009 with her partner, Rob. She can honestly say that she had never had a proper cocktail before AOC, and it was a revelation to learn that there was a whole new world of spirits to explore. AOC was followed by a few nervous visits to Clive's Classic Lounge, where she sat at tables before eventually graduating to the bar. Now she always sits at the bar, no matter where she is, and enjoys spirited conversation with those sitting beside her. Sarah loves to chat with Shawn and Nate while they whip up their custom creations and has learned a lot watching them work. In 2009, she had two or three bottles of cheap booze gathering dust under the sink. She now has over fifty bottles of premium spirits, liqueurs, and bitters as well as an eclectic collection of vintage glassware acquired from eBay and local thrift shops. All are on prominent display in her lovely teak credenza. Cookbooks are being crowded out by cocktail books and magazines, only limited by her budget and shortage of space to store them. Travelling has also taken on a new twist since that first AOC visit. Sarah now seeks out destinations with established cocktail scenes, such as Seattle, Portland, and Austin. And she always, always sits at the bar.

the bars

This section highlights the bars that we work at, drink at, and hope you will enjoy as much as we do. Each has its own style, ambience, and class, which means everyone, industry or guest, will find a spot they love. This is just the beginning of our culture here on Vancouver Island; it will continue to grow and evolve to the needs of island drinking.

The Black Hat by Bistro28

1005 Langley Street, Victoria, BC, V8W 1V7

250-381-2428

theblackhat.ca

The cocktail program at The Black Hat by Bistro28 is run by bartender Marc Wilson. The menu offers a healthy selection of approachable and classic-style cocktails. With drinks divided into Old Friends, New Friends, and Best Friends, the list ranges from well-known favourites to original creations. As with the culinary side of the restaurant, the bar puts great effort into keeping the majority of its ingredients seasonal or made in-house. Simplicity and creativity keep The Black Hat by Bistro28's cocktail program alive and thriving, putting the restaurant on the map as more than a place with great food.

Café Brio

944 Fort Street, Victoria, BC, V8V 3K2
250-383-0009
cafe-brio.com

Café Brio's menu is based on the ideology of Italian cooking: simple is best—let the quality of the food shine through. The kitchen tries to use local ingredients whenever possible and as much of that food as possible in its nose-to-tail approach to cooking. Similarly, the drink menu reflects the local.

Café Brio carries a wide selection of Vancouver Island and BC wines, as well as a large selection of handpicked international wines. Beer comes mostly from Victoria's amazing local brewers, who are true artists in the craft beer world. The cocktail program is based around the seasons and which fresh ingredients are available, as well as what people want to be drinking at that time of year. Café Brio offers something for everyone.

PHOTO BY PETE KOHUT

COURTESY OF CLIVE'S CLASSIC LOUNGE

Clive's Classic Lounge

Chateau Victoria Hotel & Suites, Lobby Level,
740 Burdett Avenue, Victoria, BC, V8W 1B2
250-361-5684
clivesclassiclounge.com

Clive's Classic Lounge breaks the stereotype of hotel bars existing solely for the exclusive use of hotel patrons. It is predominantly local clientele who frequent this bar to learn more about and appreciate the fine art of cocktails. The entire crew knows the reasons behind the bar's success and works hard to maintain the high standards they have set to support their cocktail culture and the people who embrace it. Constantly evolving is the offering of spirits, such as fine whiskies, wines, and rare beers from around the world. The always-changing drink menu, which includes complementary food pairings, keeps both frequent and occasional guests satisfied. Truly dedicated cocktail fans appreciate the calendar of recurring theme events and in-depth sessions with both guest speakers and bar staff. The overall experience is one of inclusiveness and sophisticated entertainment. Clive's, like its owner and namesake, Clive Percy, believes in quality, service, and an unwavering dedication to being the best.

Little Jumbo

102-506 Fort Street, Victoria, BC, V8R 1E6
778-433-5535
littlejumbo.ca

Little Jumbo is the latest restaurant and cocktail lounge to hit Victoria. Found down the hall, at the back of 506 Fort Street, it will be well worth the search. With its constantly rotating menus, the focus is on seasonal ingredients for the kitchen and the bar. The bar features some of the most advanced bartending equipment, such as liquid nitrogen, Perlini carbonation guns, and a self-contained hydroponic unit, along with one of the largest selections of spirits in the city. The bar showcases local beer and wine as well as a mix of classic cocktails and cocktails that use nouveau techniques. The kitchen focuses on modernized classics and features such as offal and "junk" fish, like mackerel and herring. Overall, Little Jumbo offers the highest level of cooking and bartending in a laid-back, approachable atmosphere.

PHOTO BY PETE KOHUT

LURE

Delta Victoria Ocean Pointe Resort & Spa,
45 Songhees Road, Victoria, BC, V9A 6T3
250-360-5873
lurevictoria.com

Overlooking the stunning Inner Harbour, LURE's panoramic view of downtown Victoria is unsurpassed. Located within the Delta Ocean Pointe Resort & Spa, LURE features delicious West Coast cuisine, fresh craft cocktails, and great service. Relax over breakfast, lunch, or dinner created with the island's finest local ingredients, with full gluten-free menus available.

Behind the bar, 2010 Pacific Northwest Bartending Challenge winner Dirk VanderWal and his team serve up a concise but engaging list of signature cocktails focused on fresh, high-quality ingredients, including housemade syrups, bitters, and infusions. Seasonal feature sheets allow the bartenders to use specialty ingredients when they are available and highlight their favourite flavours to complement the changing seasons. LURE is proud to feature on tap a variety of locally brewed beers from four of Victoria's best breweries. The bar's wine portfolio includes many selections from British Columbia and around the globe chosen by Jacques Lacoste, Vancouver Island's Sommelier of the Year for 2011.

Marina Restaurant

1327 Beach Drive, Victoria, BC, V8S 2N4

250-598-8555

marinarestaurant.com

Serving exceptional food and drink in a stunning oceanfront setting since 1962, the Marina Restaurant does it all. With award-winning brunch, lunch, dinner, and sushi, and an incredibly talented in-house pastry department, it can be a challenge to provide beverages to accompany all of these elements.

Two years ago, with the arrival of Brooke Levie as bar manager, followed by Cyle Serra and his refreshing herbal enthusiasm, the ante was seriously up at Marina Round Bar. Now featuring housemade syrups, bitters, cherries, and brined olives, plus fresh fruit, vegetables, and herbs, the Round Bar's drinks are seasonal, lively, and inventive. The premium spirit selection has expanded to include Japanese whisky, premium sakes, and more than 150 thoughtfully selected wines, with a strong focus on British Columbia. The bar program is simple in theory: give people what they want, and while doing that perhaps turn them on to something new, with cocktails custom-made to individual taste. From the classics to new, utterly ingenious creations, Brooke and Cyle are so devoted to their work that they have been known to look disappointed when you don't ask for something special. With passion and creativity now behind the bar, fused with stunning views and exceptional service, the Marina is truly enjoying its finest hour.

Stage Wine Bar

1307 Gladstone Avenue, Victoria, BC, V8R 1R9

250-388-4222

stagewinebar.com

Nestled in the heart of Victoria's "funky town" of Fernwood, Stage is a wine bar with an awesome array of cheeses, charcuterie, and wines by the glass. Often copied and emulated—not just in Victoria but across Canada—Stage stands alone for consistent excellence and attention to detail. Recognized as one of Canada's best new restaurants upon opening, Stage continues to surprise and delight its high-volume repeat and first-time customers. Although a wine bar, Stage serves an outstanding menu of small plates served in a tapas style to encourage tasting and wine pairing.

Of course your attention upon entering will be drawn to the bar. Made from recycled wood from a bowling alley and kept to a polished sheen, the bar is sleek, sexy, and well worth a test drive! Stage's cocktail program has been evolving over the last five years and is influenced by the classics, fresh and seasonal ingredients, and an effort to give customers something a little different to add to their dining experience. The ever-expanding liquor cupboard gives Stage's bartenders the opportunity to play around with flavour profiles and create unique, exciting cocktails. The focus at Stage is on customer service and satisfaction, so bartenders will make every effort to give the customer what they want. If you have a favourite drink, they will do their best to make it the way you like it! Stage has a small but noteworthy selection of Scotch and Irish and American whiskies, as well as a diverse collection of the more traditional alcohols, brandies, ports, and sherries (some of which end up in cocktails). They give this casual, hip room a "fine dining" touch.

The Tapa Bar

620 Trounce Alley, Victoria, BC, V8W 1K3
250-383-0013
tapabar.ca

Tucked into an alley in the downtown core, the Tapa Bar is Victoria's original small plates restaurant. The open kitchen prepares food inspired by Spain and Latin America, the room is painted with bright colours around a central arch of exposed brick, the Latin music is infectious, the cozy patio has a European feel to it, and a busy bar pumps out an array of classic and original libations. Collectively these details make for a fun, vibrant atmosphere that seems to appeal to all walks of life and caters to all types of occasions.

The Tapa Bar's restaurant has created an identity based on the idea that change isn't always the best thing; sometimes it's nice to know exactly what you're going to get. A few new items are introduced every year, but in general very little about the menu has changed in almost fifteen years of business. By contrast, the bar is where Tapa gets to be dynamic. A succinct wine list offering predominantly BC, Spanish, and

COURTESY OF THE TAPA BAR

South American wines changes a couple times a year and the beer list rotates new, local creations while maintaining a constant selection of Mexican and Spanish favourites. While all the drinks are named for Spanish artists, there is no inherent theme to the cocktails themselves. A changing list maintains a balance between innovative and accessible, so as to not alienate their clientele, and is a mix of original and classic cocktails. The most significant characteristic of the bar at Tapa is how high volume it is, so the list is designed to be creative but with drinks that can be executed en masse and under pressure. Part of the experience of sitting at the bar is watching the blur of the bartender in high-speed action.

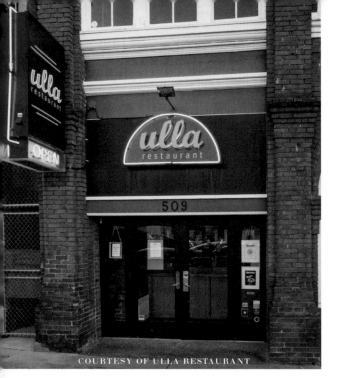

COURTESY OF ULLA RESTAURANT

ulla Restaurant

509 Fisgard Street, Victoria, BC, V8W 1R3
250-590-8795
ulla.ca

Local ingredients, classic flavours, and modern techniques sum up the philosophy at ulla. The aim of the restaurant's beverage program is to complement the food and dining experience. ulla achieves this by offering a small, well-rounded wine list selected to pair well with the menu while offering good value. A concise cocktail list consists of the classics along with seasonal concoctions developed in-house.

Veneto Tapa Lounge

1450 Douglas Street, Victoria, BC, V8W 2G1
250-383-7310
venetodining.com

Veneto Tapa Lounge is located in the
Hotel Rialto, a newly renovated heritage
landmark in downtown Victoria. Styled in
honour of the owner's Italian heritage, the
room is warm and welcoming and features
a granite bar presided over by professional bartenders. The beverage program
pays tribute to the classic spirit-forward
aesthetic of the Golden Age of the bar and
focuses on custom drink design drawing
from all ages of the craft of the cocktail.
The service team excels at working with
each individual guest to discover the perfect spirit and flavour profile called for by
the palate and the mood of the evening.

COURTESY OF VENETO TAPA LOUNGE

appendices

APPENDIX I: Housemade Ingredients

Aperol Spritz Foam

1½ oz (45 mL) Aperol
3 oz (90 mL) Prosecco
½ oz (15 mL) lemon juice
1 Tbsp (15 mL) Versawhip
pinch of xanthan gum

METHOD In a shaker tin or mixing bowl,
blend all ingredients.
Yields about 10 ounces (300 mL) of foam.

Aperol Sugar

2 cups (500 mL) white sugar
5 oz (150 mL) Aperol

METHOD Place both ingredients in a food
processor and blend thoroughly. Spread on
ungreased baking sheet and place in oven
at lowest setting (or use a dehydrator) until
mixture begins to crystalize. Once crystal-
ized and dry, return to food processor and
blitz several times. Put through a sieve to
remove larger particles. Use a mortar and
pestle to make the larger pieces fine enough
to pass through the sieve.

Apple Cinnamon Vodka

3 cups (750 mL) vodka
2 red apples, cored and peeled
8 to 10 cinnamon sticks

METHOD Place all ingredients in an airtight
jar and let infuse for 1 week, shaking the
jar once a day. After 1 week, double-strain
vodka through a fine mesh strainer and a
coffee filter. Bottle and enjoy.

Cardamom & Pomegranate Ice Cubes

¼ cup (60 mL) cardamom pods
3 cups (750 mL) POM pomegranate juice

METHOD In a dry pan on low heat, toast pods
for 20 minutes, then transfer to a Mason
jar and add POM juice. Infuse for 2 days
before straining into ice cube trays and
freezing.

Cardamom Syrup

½ cup (125 mL) green cardamom pods
2 cups (500 mL) white sugar
2 cups (500 mL) water

METHOD Crush cardamom pods with a
muddler, or use a mortar and pestle. In a
saucepan, combine crushed pods with sugar
and water. Bring to a boil, then remove from
heat and allow to cool to room temperature
(approximately 90 minutes). Double-strain
out solids and store in the refrigerator.

Cherry Brandy

2 cups (500 mL) brandy
1 cup (250 mL) Luxardo Maraschino
1 lb (500 g) Morello cherries

METHOD Use quality cherries in this recipe.
Obviously fresh is best, but preservative-
free canned is a good alternative.

In an airtight container, pour brandy
and maraschino liqueur. Add cherries and
seal container. Let infuse for 1 month, shaking weekly. Double-strain and bottle liquid,
reserving cherries for another use.

Cinnamon Bitters

cinnamon sticks
black peppercorns
cloves
star anise
2 cups (500 mL) vodka

METHOD Fill a large sterilized Mason jar
with cinnamon sticks, making sure they get
packed in tight. Add some black peppercorns, cloves, and star anise, then top with
vodka until spices are all covered. Place jar
in a dark space, and shake daily for about a
month, until liquid is dark brown and rich
in cinnamon aroma. Check developing flavour periodically. Double-strain into bottles
through a doubled-up cheesecloth.

Cinnamon Smoked Madeira

1 bottle (750 mL) Madeira (Blandy's Madeira)
2 cinnamon sticks, pestled

METHOD You will need a PolyScience
  Smoking Gun.
    Pour Madeira into a large (bigger than
  2 L) Mason jar. Place tube of cold smoker
  into jar. Pack pestled cinnamon sticks into
  hopper of smoking gun and light—you will
  need to keep the flame on the cinnamon
  until it glows. Smoke should be coming out
  of the end of the tube into the liquid. Blow
  a bit of excess smoke onto the surface of the
  Madeira and cap the Mason jar. Shake the
  smoke through the liquid and let sit for 5 to
  10 minutes. Repeat smoking process at least
  3 times. The final product should have a distinct flavour of smoky cinnamon.
    Yields 1 bottle (750 mL).

Cinnamon Syrup

4 cups (1 L) water
6 cups (1.5 L) white sugar
5 cinnamon sticks

METHOD In a pot over medium heat, combine all ingredients and simmer for about
  30 minutes, until sugar has dissolved and
  cinnamon has infused the syrup. Pour syrup,
  including a few of the cinnamon sticks, into
  a bottle and refrigerate for up to 2 months.

Clarified Lime Peel Syrup

4 cups (1 L) water, at room temperature
peel from 3 limes
2 lbs (1 kg) white sugar

METHOD Steep lime peels in water overnight.
  Filter through coffee filters twice to remove
  majority of sediment and colour. Add liquid
  to a pot and bring to a simmer, then add
  sugar and stir until dissolved.

Clove Syrup

4 cups (1 L) water
6 cups (1.5 L) white sugar
handful cloves

METHOD In a pot over medium heat, combine all ingredients and simmer for about
  30 minutes, until sugar has dissolved and
  cloves have infused the syrup. Pour syrup,
  including the cloves, into a bottle and refrigerate for up to 2 months.

Cola Syrup

zest from 4 oranges
zest from 4 limes
zest from 2 lemons
1 tsp (5 mL) ground cinnamon
1 tsp (5 mL) ground nutmeg
4 star anise
1 tsp (5 mL) lavender buds
2 tsp (10 mL) kola nut powder
1 tsp (5 mL) ground ginger
half a vanilla bean, seeds removed
4 cups (1 L) water
½ tsp (2 mL) citric acid
2 lb (1 kg) turbinado sugar

METHOD In a saucepan on an induction burner, combine all ingredients except sugar and heat over medium-low for 25 to 30 minutes. Remove from heat and strain. Return to same heat and add sugar. Heat until sugar dissolves, about 15 minutes, then bottle.

Cranberry Syrup

2 cups (500 mL) fresh cranberries
2 cups (500 mL) white sugar
8 cups (2 L) water

METHOD Place ingredients in a pan and simmer for approximately 20 to 30 minutes. Double-strain and bottle. Keeps for 1 month.

Driftwood Singularity Reduction

26 oz (750 mL) bottle Driftwood Singularity Russian Imperial Stout

METHOD Pour beer into a heavy-bottomed pan. Let stand uncovered for a few hours to get rid of the carbonation. (Stirring helps.) Bring to a gentle simmer and let reduce until a concentrated syrup consistency is achieved, about 30 to 40 minutes.
Yields about 7 ounces (210 mL).

Earl Grey Tea Syrup

4 cups (1 L) freshly brewed loose-leaf Earl Grey tea
6 cups (1.5 L) white sugar

METHOD In a pot over low heat, combine Earl Grey tea and sugar. Gently simmer to dissolve the sugar, then bottle and refrigerate for up to 2 months.

Espresso Syrup

⅕ lb (100 g) good-quality coffee beans, coarsely ground
½ lb (250 g) white sugar

METHOD In a French press, place grounds and add hot water. The grounds will float to the top and form a crust. At the 1 minute mark, break the crust and stir. Steep for a further 3 minutes and then plunge the filter. Pour coffee over sugar and stir vigorously until sugar is dissolved. Bottle and store for up to 1 month.

Gentian & Wormwood Tincture

3⅓ oz (100 mL) vodka
2 tsp (10 mL) dried gentian
2 tsp (10 mL) dried wormwood

METHOD In a Mason jar, combine ingredients. Screw on the lid. Let stand for 2 weeks, shaking every few days. Double-strain and store.

Ginger & Honey Shrub

1 cup (250 mL) peeled and chopped ginger
5 oz (150 mL) honey
10 oz (300 mL) hot water
4 cups (1 L) white sugar
10 oz (300 mL) rice wine vinegar

METHOD Place ginger, honey, and hot water in a food processor. Blend into a paste, then pour into a pot on an induction burner. Add sugar and rice wine vinegar and simmer over medium-low for 15 minutes. Pour unstrained into a bottle.

Ginger Infused Gin

½ cup (125 mL) peeled and finely diced ginger
3 cups (750 mL) gin

METHOD Add ingredients to a Mason jar and screw on lid. Let stand for 2 weeks, shaking daily. Fine double-strain and then rebottle.

Ginger Syrup

2 cups (500 mL) white sugar
1 cup (250 mL) water
¾ cup (185 mL) peeled fresh ginger

METHOD In a saucepan, incorporate all
ingredients until sugar dissolves. Bring to
a simmer while stirring constantly, then
remove from heat. Double-strain and let cool
to room temperature before refrigerating.

Gomme Syrup

2 oz (60 mL) gum arabic
6 oz (180 mL) water, divided
1 cup (250 mL) white sugar

METHOD Use refined gum arabic, which
should be available as a white powder; do
not use the chunks you have to grind into
powder.

In a small bowl, combine gum arabic
with 2 oz (60 mL) water and let stand overnight, until gum arabic is fully hydrated. In
a small pot, dissolve sugar in remaining 4 oz
(120 mL) of water and bring to a boil. Add
hydrated gum arabic and whisk it into the
hot syrup until dissolved. Skim off any foam.
Double-strain and cool before using.

Grand Fir Tincture

⅙ oz (5 g) grand fir needles
1¼ cup (310 mL) 40% ABV neutral grain spirit

METHOD In a sealed container, allow needles
to infuse alcohol for 30 days, agitating daily.
Double-strain through cheesecloth, wringing
all excess liquid from the needles.

Green Tea & Serrano Chili Amaro

2 serrano chilies
3 cups (750 mL) vodka
4 tsp (20 mL) green tea (dry tea leaves)
4 oz (120 mL) agave syrup, or to taste
½ oz (15 mL) Gentian & Wormwood Tincture
(p. 177)

METHOD In a Mason jar, place chilies and
vodka and let stand for about 5 hours.
Double-strain liquid into a clean Mason
jar. Add green tea and let stand for 3 hours.
Fine double-strain and add agave syrup
and tincture.

Grilled Cheese Washed Mount Gay Rum

2 grilled cheese sandwiches made with
    sourdough bread
3 cups (750 mL) Mount Gay Rum

METHOD Place ingredients into a Mason jar.
    Let stand for 24 hours. Double-strain the
    liquid into a sealable container and freeze
    for about 1 hour (doing so will freeze the fat
    in the liquid but not the liquor). Double-
    strain through a coffee filter to remove any
    leftover sediment.

Hibiscus Liqueur

1¾ oz (50 g) dried hibiscus flowers
3 cups (750 mL) vodka
1½ cups (375 mL) Gomme Syrup (p. 178)

METHOD Use good-quality vodka for this
    recipe. We recommend 42 Below.
       In a sealable jar, place hibiscus flowers
    and vodka. Let stand for 1 week to infuse.
    Double-strain and cut with syrup.

Honey & Lemongrass Syrup

2 oz (60 g) finely chopped fresh lemongrass
2¼ oz (65 g) peeled fresh ginger, roughly chopped
2 cups (500 mL) honey

METHOD In a saucepan, combine lemongrass
    and ginger with 2 cups (500 mL) water.
    Simmer for 15 minutes. Remove from heat
    and cover; let steep for 6 hours. Strain out
    solids and add honey to make syrup.

Honey Syrup

1 cup (250 mL) honey
1 cup (250 mL) boiling water

METHOD In a jug, combine honey and water
    and mix thoroughly, until a thin consistency
    is achieved.

Honey Tea Ginger Syrup

¼ cup (60 mL) diced fresh ginger
4 tea bags orange pekoe tea
1 cup (250 mL) boiling water
¾ cup (185 mL) honey

METHOD Place ginger and tea bags in a mea-
    suring cup or mixing glass and add boiling
    water. Let steep for 10 to 15 minutes. While
    water is still warm, gently press on tea bags
    and ginger to extract their flavour, then
    double-strain. Stir honey into the liquid.

Housemade Limoncello

6 medium lemons
3 cups (750 mL) vodka, divided
1 cup (250 mL) white sugar
1 cup (250 mL) water

METHOD Wash lemons. Use a grater or zester to remove the zest, reserving the lemons for another use. Place lemon zest in a jar, add half of the vodka, and let steep in a dark place for at least 2 weeks. Shake daily. Double-strain into a bowl through a doubled-up and moistened cheesecloth, making sure to squeeze out all the goodness from the zest. Add the remaining vodka. In a saucepan over medium-high heat, dissolve sugar in water. Remove from heat and let cool. Just before it has completely cooled, add sugar water to vodka infusion. Use a funnel to pour mixture into sterilized containers and let sit for 1 more week to allow all of the flavours to integrate.

Lemongrass Syrup

4 stalks lemongrass
2 cups (500 mL) white sugar
1 cup (250 mL) water

METHOD Using the back of a cleaver or chef's knife, bruise lemongrass. In a saucepan, incorporate all ingredients. Bring to a simmer while stirring constantly and then remove from heat. Double-strain and let cool to room temperature before refrigerating.

Lime & Eucalyptus Crushed Ice

1½ cups (375 mL) lime juice
1½ cups (375 mL) water
5 drops eucalyptus citriodora oil

METHOD Mix ingredients together and pour into an ice cube mould. Freeze and then crush using a hammer and Lewis bag, food processor, or ice crusher.

Morel Mushroom Infused Bourbon

1 lb (500 g) fresh morel mushrooms
26 oz (750 mL) bourbon whiskey (Bulleit)

METHOD Dry-roast morels in the oven at 350°F (180°C) for about 10 minutes to remove any extra moisture. In a sealable glass jar, combine morels and bourbon. Place jar in a pot of simmering water. Let infuse for about 1 hour, then strain contents through cheesecloth. Allow bourbon to cool before using.

Orange Cinnamon Tincture

peels from 5 oranges
5 cinnamon sticks
4 cups (1 L) vodka, divided

METHOD Use good-quality vodka for this recipe; overproof is preferable.

Dehydrate orange peels overnight. Place peels in one Mason jar and cinnamon sticks in another. Add half of the vodka to each jar, seal jars, and let sit for 1 week, shaking daily. Double-strain both batches and blend to taste.

Pekoe Infused Bourbon

2 Tbsp (30 mL) orange pekoe tea (dry tea leaves)
3 cups (750 mL) Bulleit Bourbon

METHOD Place ingredients in a jar and let steep for a few hours (tea infusions are very quick). Double-strain and rebottle.

Phillips Amnesiac IPA Reduction

26 oz (750 mL) bottle Phillips Amnesiac IPA

METHOD Pour beer into a heavy-bottomed pan. Let stand uncovered for a few hours to get rid of the carbonation. (Stirring helps.) Bring to a gentle simmer and let reduce until a concentrated syrup consistency is achieved, about 30 to 40 minutes.

Yields about 7 ounces (210 mL).

Pineapple Syrup

8 cups (2 L) pineapple juice
2 cups (500 mL) white sugar

METHOD In a saucepan, pour juice and sugar; let simmer for approximately 20 to 30 minutes. Double-strain and bottle. Keeps for 1 month.

Rhubarb Syrup

5 stalks rhubarb, chopped
2 cups (500 mL) Sugar Syrup (p. 183)

METHOD Frozen rhubarb that has been
thawed works best for this recipe.
    Place rhubarb in a food processor and
blitz. Add syrup and double-strain through
a fine strainer. Refrigerate and keep for up
to 1 month.

Rosemary Syrup

½ cup (125 mL) water
½ cup (125 mL) white sugar
5 sprigs fresh rosemary

METHOD In a small pot on the stove, heat
up the water and sugar until the sugar dissolves. Add rosemary sprigs and let them
cook for about 2 minutes. Remove pot from
heat and let sit for at least 5 minutes. Allow
mixture to cool and then strain.

Sarsaparilla Syrup

2 Tbsp (30 mL) dried sassafras root
2 tsp (10 mL) sarsaparilla
2 tsp (10 mL) dried burdock root
2 tsp (10 mL) dried licorice root
5 or 6 tongues dried astragalus root
4 cups (1 L) filtered water
1½ cups (375 mL) brown sugar

METHOD In a pot, place herbs and water,
bring to a boil, and let simmer until reduced
by half. Let stand for 2 hours. Reheat and
add sugar, stirring until dissolved.

Saskatoon Liqueur

3 cups (750 mL) vodka
2 cups (500 mL) Saskatoon berries
2 cups (500 mL) Saskatoon berry juice
4 oz (120 mL) Gomme Syrup (p. 178)

METHOD Pour vodka in a jar; add Saskatoon
berries. Allow to infuse for 3 days, then
blitz in a food processor. Let infuse for a
further 4 days. Double-strain through a
coffee filter, then cut with Saskatoon juice
and Gomme Syrup.

Silk Road Spicy Mandarin Syrup

3 Tbsp (45 mL) Silk Road Spicy Mandarin Tea
(dry tea leaves)
1 cup (250 mL) boiling water
¾ cup (185 mL) organic light brown sugar

METHOD Combine tea with boiling water. Let
steep for 5 minutes, then double-strain into
a pot. Add sugar and combine. Simmer until
sugar is dissolved. Chill syrup before storing
in a clean glass jar in the fridge.

Spiced Syrup

4 cups (1 L) water
6 cups (1.5 L) white sugar
5 cinnamon sticks
handful cloves
6 star anise
half a handful Szechuan peppercorns

METHOD In a pot over medium heat, combine all ingredients and simmer for about
30 minutes, until sugar has dissolved and
flavours have infused the syrup. Pour syrup,
including the spices, into a bottle and refrigerate for up to 2 months.

Sugar Syrup

3 cups (750 mL) white sugar
4 cups (1 L) water

METHOD In a pot, combine sugar and water.
Bring to a simmer and let reduce for 30 minutes, making sure not to let mixture boil.

Sugar Syrup - Quick Method

5½ cups (1.375 L) white sugar
4 cups (1 L) boiling water

METHOD In a jug, combine sugar and water.
Stir until sugar is dissolved.

Switchel

15 cups (3.75 L) water, divided
½ cup (125 mL) apple cider vinegar
1½ cups (375 mL) white sugar
2¾ oz (82.5 mL) light or fancy molasses
2 oz (60 mL) grated fresh ginger

METHOD Combine 4 cups (1 L) of the water
with vinegar, sugar, molasses, and ginger, and
simmer uncovered for 30 minutes. Remove
from heat, cover, and allow to cool for 30 minutes. Pour slowly into a glass jug containing
the remaining 11 cups (2.75 L) of water. Add
additional water to make 1 gallon (4 L).

Thyme Soda

10 large sprigs fresh thyme
sugar syrup

METHOD Use a sugar syrup like the one on
this page, but made with a 1:1 ratio of sugar
to water. In a saucepan over medium heat,
simmer thyme in syrup for 15 minutes. Remove
from heat and let cool in a sealed container.
    Add 3 ounces (90 mL) of thyme syrup
to a soda siphon or SodaStream Bottle. Fill
siphon/bottle with water and carbonate.

APPENDIX II: Sourcing Ingredients on Vancouver Island

Cascadia Liquor Stores

Quadra Village

2631 Quadra Street, Victoria, BC, V8T 4E3

250-590-1940

Colwood / Hatley Park

Hatley Park Plaza, 2244 Sooke Road, Colwood, BC, V9B 2A6

250-478-1303

cascadialiquor.com

One of the best liquor stores in Victoria, they have worked hard to build up their selection of "geek" spirits.

Charelli's Cheese Shop & Delicatessen

2851 Foul Bay Road, Victoria, BC, V8R 5G5

250-598-4794

charellis.com

A great source for local bitters, syrups, and oddities for the cocktail world. They sell Peychaud's, Regans' Orange Bitters, and the Bitter Truth range along with shrubs, syrups, and boutique sodas.

Hillside Liquor Store

3201 Shelbourne Street, Victoria, BC, V8P 5G9

250-370-1143

hillsideliquorstore.com

A relative newcomer to the cocktail "geek" scene, they landed fast and hard with their collection of Bittermens bitters and specialty liquors.

Ottavio Italian Bakery & Delicatessen

2272 Oak Ave Bay Avenue, Victoria, BC, V8R 1G4

250-592-4080

ottaviovictoria.com

The ultimate source for exotic Italian sodas, Fee Brothers bitters, and various hard-to-find syrups.

Self Heal Herbs

1106 Blanshard Street, Victoria, BC, V8W 2H6

250-383-1913

Victoria's best kept secret for all sorts of weird herbs, spices, and roots. A one-stop shop for some of the harder-to-find ingredients in our recipes.

The Strath Liquor Store

919 Douglas Street, Victoria, BC, V8W 2C2

250-370-9463

strathconahotel.com/TheStrathLiquorStore.aspx

The Strath has one of the largest selections of whiskies in Victoria.

APPENDIX III: Online Sources and Blogs

@bayareaspirits #handcrafted #imbibe

bayareaspirits.com

The David-vs.-Goliath blog that focuses on craft distillers and artisanal, handcrafted, and hard-to-find spirits and cocktails.

Alcademics

alcademics.com

Camper English is a San Francisco-based freelance writer and consultant who specializes in cocktails and spirits, with a touch of travel thrown in.

Art of Drink

artofdrink.com

Darcy O'Neil's blog was spontaneously created in October 2005 as a way to document information on all things drink-related. Currently, Art of Drink is ranked among the top, if not the top, cocktail blogs on the Internet.

The Barkeeper

thebarkeeper.com

Don't forget to pay Uncle Brian a visit. Brian Rea has stuff on his blog that you'll never find anywhere else in the world. Don't say we didn't tell you.

Bar Products

barproducts.com

If you need anything from spoons to tiki mugs, this is the place to go!

Booze Business

boozebusiness.com

Our old friend Arthur Shapiro spills some fabulous booze-related tales on his blog. Go pay him a visit.

The Cocktail Chronicles

cocktailchronicles.com

Updated somewhat regularly by Paul Clarke, a Seattle-based cocktail enthusiast. He's taken David Embury's "roll your own" ethic to heart, spending countless hours reading about, mixing, and studying an array of cocktails, with a special emphasis on early and mid-twentieth-century classics.

The Cocktail Guru

thecocktailguru.com

Want to see what Jonathan Pogash is up to this week? Go worship here.

Cocktail Kingdom

cocktailkingdom.com

Your one-stop shop for all things "geek," including tools, reproduction cocktail books, bitters, and syrups.

Drinks Ink

drinksink.blogspot.com

Wherein a sharp-tongued boozehound (Jack Robertiello) shares what he thinks about what he drinks, among other things.

Fork & Shaker

forkandshaker.com

Blogger Naren Young says: "Fork & Shaker is a metaphor for two of my great passions in life—food and drink. Maybe this site will make you thirsty. Maybe it will make you hungry. Maybe it will show you that the world of cocktails and other fine libations can be found all over the world. But if it does nothing more than help you appreciate all that is beautiful and unique when the crossroads of food and drink meet, then that will make me very happy."

gaz regan

gazregan.com

Ramblings from one of our most favourite people in the world, gaz regan. He swears, yells, and insults, but at the end of the day, he has a heart of gold and will do anything for you. A true champion bartender.

Good Spirits News

goodspiritsnews.com

Reports on the latest trends in mixology from around the world. Reviews of spirits, liqueurs, bitters, and the best new spirited publications, as well as information about bartender competitions and cocktail events. The site also includes interviews with the likes of gaz regan, F. Paul Pacult, and Dave Wondrich, to name but a few.

House Made

housemade.ca

The home of Victoria's local bitters and syrups queen, Janice Mansfield. She went from being an at-home enthusiast to launching her own line of bitters a few years ago.

Imbibe magazine

imbibemagazine.com

The source for news about what's going on in the cocktail world and for the big trends in the United States right now. A go-to guide of everything needed for bartending.

Jeffrey Morgenthaler

jeffreymorgenthaler.com

Jeffrey writes about bartending and mixology from Portland, Oregon.

The Jerry Thomas Project

thejerrythomasproject.blogspot.ca

The re-creation of all of the cocktails from Jerry Thomas's *The Bartender's Guide: How to Mix Drinks* in their purest form.

The Liquid Muse

theliquidmuse.com

Launched in 2006 by Natalie Bovis, a cocktail book
author, freelance writer, and mixologist. With
twenty years experience in front-of-the-house
hospitality, Natalie now shares her favourite
cocktail bars, spirits, and wines from around the
world via her website.

Professor Cocktail

professorcocktail.com

The not-so-secret identity of David J. Montgomery,
professional book critic by day, amateur cocktail-
ian by night.

Small Screen

smallscreennetwork.com

This vlog based out of Seattle showcases some of
the best and brightest bartenders in the Pacific
Northwest and across the United States. Great
visuals and high-quality filmography.

Spirits and Cocktails

spiritsandcocktails.com

Jamie Boudreau's thirst for cocktail minutia is infamous. If the conversation turns to a subject he
is unsure of, you can bet he will research it as
soon as possible. He loves the classics, but at
the same time is always looking for new, exciting
ingredients to try in new recipes.

Spirits Review

spiritsreview.com

Reviews of booze, books, and barware. With 4,500+
links, 400+ RSS feeds, and an extensive
"Adventure" section chronicling adventures in
alcohol in various forms, this site aims to be "the
Google of booze."

drinks by difficulty

Beverage Formerly Known as Glo Refresh, The
Canes & Coatails
Cannibal's Campfire
Centennial
Clover Point, The
Crouching Tiger
Cynar Crusta
Dawn's Reward
Fernadito Flip
Five Magics
Good Ju Ju
Grown Up Roy Rogers
High Jack
Holy Hand Grenade
Honolulu Ink Flip
Humboldt
Jamaican Sazerac
Jessica Rabbit
Kamikaze Carrot
Kentucky P'ale
Kilt in the Monastery
Koala Mojito
Managua
Maria Full of Grace
Morel Disposition
Moscow Monk
Normandy Swizzle
Nymph's Reply, The
Peko Bou
Pop the Strawberry
Reverse Cosmosis
Rhubarb Fizz
Rosemary's Baby
Sevilla Sunrise
Sherry Bobbins

Tar Pit
Tequila North
Treacle de Lux
Tsar, The
Velvet Underground, The

Ÿ Ÿ Ÿ
Albino Hemingway Daiquiri
Bellucci
Burning Bridges
Chestnut Cabinet
Click Your Heels Thrice
Cold Night In
Flip the Switch
Golden Age, The
Hemming Gucci
Invierno de Jerez
Jamaican Switch
Lazimon's Sorrel Rum Punch
Mayahuel Flame
Old Thyme Prairie Berry Fizz
Paradisi
PDX
Pop Top Collins
Rum Plum Sour
Sarsaparilla Julep
Saskatoon Julep
Satchmo
Shiso Sour
Sugar Shack, The
Tree de Vie
Versailles Spice

glossary

absinthe: A green liqueur flavoured with wormwood (or a substitute), anise, and other aromatics.

ABV: Stands for alcohol by volume. A standard measure of how much alcohol (ethanol) there is in an alcoholic beverage (expressed as a percentage of total volume). This standard is used worldwide.

acid phosphate: Gives a drink sourness without making it taste like anything in particular. Its inherent salts can enhance existing flavours, much as salt does with food.

Adonis: A Fino Sherry–based cocktail dating back to the late 1800s. Named after a Broadway play that ran for over five hundred shows.

agave syrup: Made from the nectar of the agave plant, it can be used as an alternative sweetener in place of maple syrup, honey, or standard refined sugar.

akvavit: A strong, clear Scandinavian liquor distilled from potato or grain mash and flavoured with caraway seed and dill.

amaro: Italian for "bitter." An Italian herbal liqueur that is commonly consumed as an after-dinner digestif. It usually has a bittersweet flavour, is sometimes syrupy, and has an alcohol content between 16 and 35 percent.

amaretto: An Italian liqueur flavoured with almonds.

añejo rum: Aged rum. There are no legal definitions of what "aged" means; however, there are a few countries that have minimum aging requirements for rum production. For instance, Puerto Rico requires one year and Venezuela requires two.

Angostura Bitters: Aromatic bitters with flavours of gentian, clove, and allspice, most famously used in the Manhattan and the Old Fashioned.

Aperol: An Italian aperitif originally produced by the Barbieri Brothers, a company based in Padua. Aperol is now produced by the Campari company. Though it was created in 1919, Aperol did not become successful until after the Second World War. Its ingredients include, among others, bitter orange, gentian, rhubarb, and cinchona. It has an alcohol content of 11 percent.

aromatic bitters: Bitters that contain aromatic oils but few tannins.

atomizer: A device for emitting water, perfume, or other liquids as a fine spray.

Benedictine: A liqueur containing aromatic herbs and spices, originally made by Benedictine monks in France.

blackstrap rum: Rum made with dark, viscous molasses, the by-product of the final extraction phase of sugar-refining.

blended whisk(e)y: Whisky that is either a blend of two or more whiskies, especially a malt whisky and an unmalted grain whisky, or a blend of whisky and other neutral spirits.

Boulevardier: A cocktail that is part of the Negroni family. It uses the same ingredients but is fortified with more bourbon. First published in Harry McElhone's 1927 cocktail book *Barflies and Cocktails*.

bourbon whiskey: American whiskey that must consist of at least 51 percent corn, be aged in new charred-oak barrels at a minimum of 62.5 percent ABV, and be bottled at no less than 40 percent ABV. Made predominantly in Kentucky.

Brooklyn: One of the New York borough cocktails, the most famous of which is, of course, the Manhattan. The Brooklyn is a twist on the basic DNA of the Manhattan. It uses rye, dry vermouth, maraschino liqueur, and one of the rarest liqueurs in the world, Amer Picon. Amer Picon is a French amer/amaro that has limited exportation throughout the world outside of France.

cachaça: Brazil's national spirit. Similar to rum but distilled from sugar cane juice rather than molasses.

Caipirinha: One of the best-selling drinks in Brazil. A mix of fresh, muddled lime, sugar (syrup or granulated), and cachaça.

calvados: A dry apple brandy made in Normandy, France.

Campari: An alcoholic aperitif made by infusing herbs and fruit (including chinotto and cascarilla) in alcohol and water. It is characterized by its dark red colour.

channelled lemon twist: A thicker spiral of lemon zest cut with a channel knife.

Chartreuse: An aromatic green or yellow liqueur flavoured with orange peel, hyssop, and peppermint oils. Made at a monastery near Grenoble, France.

citric acid: A sharp-tasting crystalline acid, present in the juice of lemons and other sour fruits. It is a natural preservative and is used to add an acidic, or sour, taste to foods and drinks.

Cocktail à la Louisiane: In Stanley Clisby Arthur's book *Famous New Orleans Drinks and How to Mix 'Em*, published in 1937, he explained that the Cocktail à la Louisiane was the house cocktail at the Restaurant de la Louisiane, "one of the famous French restaurants in New Orleans, long the rendezvous of those who appreciate the best in Creole cuisine." The cocktail uses rye, sweet vermouth, and Benedictine, with hints of absinthe or Herbsaint and dashes of Peychaud's bitters.

Collins: An iced drink made with gin (Tom Collins) or vodka, rum, whisk(e)y, etc., mixed with soda water, lime or lemon juice, and sugar. Also a style of tall glass.

cordial: A strong, highly flavoured sweet liquor usually consumed after a meal.

crème de cacao: A sweet liqueur flavoured with vanilla and cacao beans.

crème de cassis: A sweet, dark red liqueur made from blackcurrants.

Crusta: By definition can have any spirit as its base. It is a particular small style of drink, which seems to require two things to make it legitimate: a frosted wine glass rimmed with sugar and the entire peel of a lemon or orange fitted into the glass.

Cynar: An Italian bitter liqueur made from thirteen herbs and plants, predominantly the artichoke (*Cynara scolymus*), from which the drink derives its name.

dark rum: Aged longer than clear white rum, usually in heavily charred oak barrels. It also possesses a far greater flavour than white rum or even gold rum, usually with a sweeter taste.

drinking vinegar: Certain vinegars (apple cider, for example) can be used as a daily tonic to change the body's pH from acidic to alkaline.

dry vermouth: A fortified white wine, usually 18 percent alcohol (36 proof), that contains at most 5 percent residual sugar. It's consumed as an aperitif and is a vital part of the dry martini.

Elixir Végétal: Made from the same base of about 130 medicinal and aromatic plants and flowers as Chartreuse, but far stronger. It can be described as a cordial or a liqueur and is claimed to be a tonic. Sold in small bottles placed in wooden casing.

falernum: A sweet syrup used in Caribbean and tropical drinks. It contains flavours of almond, ginger and/or cloves, lime, and sometimes vanilla or allspice.

fat washing: A method of infusing liquor with a fatty product, usually meat.

Fernet-Branca: Long known as a digestif, it originated in Milan in the early 1800s. As with most such elixirs, it is made from a secret formula. This one purportedly includes some forty ingredients, including rhubarb, chamomile, and myrrh.

Fino Sherry: A pale, very dry sherry produced in Jerez, Spain.

fizz: A type of mixed drink; a variation on the older sours family. The defining features of the fizz are an acidic juice (such as lemon or lime juice) and carbonated water.

flip: A chilled, creamy drink made with eggs, sugar, and a wine or spirit (brandy and sherry are two of the most common choices).

float: (verb/noun) Adding a liquid or foam to a drink without turbulence or mixing. The addition should be a distinct layer sitting on top of the other components of the cocktail.

foam: Foams can be made a few different ways using Versawhip (p. 173) or egg whites. You can shake the foam with the cocktail to create a frothy drink, or you can make it separately in a whipped cream canister and then add it to the top of the drink. The addition of flavours to foams, egg white or other, adds a new texture and dimension to a drink because the cocktail is sipped through the flavoured foam.

Frangelico: A hazelnut and herbal liqueur produced in Canale, Italy. It is 20 percent ABV, 40 proof. It was released in the 1980s, gaining attention largely because of its unusual packaging: its bottle was designed to look like a friar, complete with a knotted white cord around the waist. Frangelico is made in a similar manner to some other nut liqueurs. Nuts are crumbled up and combined with cocoa, vanilla berries, and other natural flavours, then left to soak in the base spirit. After the spirit has absorbed the flavour of the ingredients, the liqueur is filtered, sweetened, and bottled.

Galliano: A sweet herbal liqueur created in 1896 by Italian distiller and brandy producer Arturo Vaccari of Livorno, Tuscany, and named after Giuseppe Galliano, an Italian hero of the First Italo-Ethiopian War. Its vivid yellow colour symbolizes the gold rushes of the 1890s. Galliano has a large number of natural ingredients including vanilla, star anise, Mediterranean anise, ginger, citrus, juniper, musk yarrow, and lavender. Neutral alcohol is infused with the pressings from all the herbs except vanilla. The liquid is then distilled and infused with pressed vanilla. In the final stage, distilled water, refined sugar, and pure neutral alcohol are blended with the base.

gentian: The roots of a yellow-petalled flower found in southern Europe that are dried and used as a tonic, stomachic, and flavouring in vermouth.

ginger disc: A thin slice of ginger resembling a disc.

gold rum: Rum that has been aged in oak barrels, which give it a golden colour. Usually has a slightly deeper and more complex flavour than white rum. Also called amber rum.

gomme syrup: Rich simple sugar syrup with the addition of gum arabic.

grenadine: A red syrup created by combining various berry juices and sugar. Most commonly, though, pomegranate juice is the main ingredient.

gum arabic: The hardened sap from Acacia trees. Used as a stabilizer and thickening agent. Also known as acacia gum.

Heering Cherry: Danish cherry liqueur that has been made since 1818. Used most notably in the Singapore Sling and the Blood & Sand.

Herbsaint: Herbsaint first appeared in 1934. It was the creation of J. Marion Legendre and Reginald Parker of New Orleans, who had learned how to make absinthe while in France during the First World War. It first went on sale as a substitute for absinthe following the repeal of Prohibition. Herbsaint was originally produced under the name "Legendre Absinthe," although it never contained grand wormwood (*Artemisia absinthium*). The Federal Alcohol Control Administration soon objected to Legendre's use of the word "absinthe," so the name was changed to "Legendre Herbsaint." The Sazerac Company bought J.M. Legendre & Co. in June 1949. Herbsaint was bottled at 120 proof and 100 proof for many years, but when the recipe was modified in the mid-1950s, it began being bottled at 100 proof and 90 proof. By the early 1970s, the 100 proof variation was discontinued, and the 90 proof version remains the predominant Herbsaint available today. In December 2009, the Sazerac Company reintroduced J.M. Legendre's original

100 proof recipe as Herbsaint Original. The name Herbsaint originates from "herbe sainte" (sacred herb), the French/Creole term for *Artemisia absinthium*.

housemade: (adjective) Anything that's been made by the bar for use in drinks. Specialty syrups and liqueurs are often housemade.

House Made: A small bitters and syrup company based in Victoria, BC, and run by Janice Mansfield.

Hpnotiq: A fruit juice liqueur with a base of vodka and cognac. Native to New York but produced in France by Heaven Hill Distilleries.

ice globe: Ice shaped into a globe or sphere using a specialty mould, carving technique, or ice globe press.

infuse: (verb) To let ingredients sit in alcohol for a prolonged period of time, allowing flavours to release into the liquid.

Islay whisky: Home to only eight distilleries, Islay is one of the smallest of the Scottish whisky regions. Produces notably smokier whiskies than other regions due to the use of local peat to smoke the malts.

kirsch: A clear, colourless fruit brandy traditionally made from a double distillation of Morello cherries. It can, however, be made from other varieties. The cherries are fermented completely, even the pits. Good-quality kirsch will have a dry cherry flavour with a slightly bitter almond taste.

kola nut powder: The powder derived from the nuts of the Cola trees of Africa. One of the original caffeine and flavour ingredients in old-school colas.

Last Word: A gin-based Prohibition-era cocktail written about by Ted Saucier, a Canadian icon in the cocktail scene. A mix of equal parts gin, maraschino, Green Chartreuse, and lime juice. Resurrected by Murray Stenson in Seattle.

Lillet Blanc: Lillet is a brand of French aperitif wine. It is a blend of 85 percent Bordeaux wines (Sauvignon Blanc, Sémillon, and Muscadelle) and 15 percent macerated liqueurs, mostly citrus liqueurs made from the peels of sweet oranges from Spain and Morocco and bitter green oranges from Haiti. Lillet belongs to a family of aperitif known as tonic wines because of the addition of a liqueur of cinchona bark from Peru, which contains quinine. Lillet is matured in oak casks and available in red and white versions. While it had been produced since the late nineteenth century under the name Kina Lillet, the current formulation, called Lillet Blanc, dates from 1986, when the formulation was changed to lower the sugar content and bitterness.

London dry gin: The most classic style of gin available, resulting from the infusion and redistillation of various botanicals, with juniper berries being predominant.

Madeira: Madeira is a proprietary fortified wine from Madeira, Portugal. Madeira can be made in two styles: dry aperitif or sweeter dessert. It is produced using the unique *estufagem* aging process, which is meant to duplicate the effect of a long sea voyage through tropical climates on the aging barrels.

Mai Tai: It was purportedly invented at the Trader Vic's restaurant in Oakland, California, in

1944. Trader Vic's rival, Don the Beachcomber, claimed to have created it in 1933 at his then-new Hollywood bar, which he named after himself (it is now a famous restaurant). Don the Beachcomber's recipe is more complex than Vic's and tastes quite different.

The Trader Vic story of its invention is that the Trader (Victor J. Bergeron) created it one afternoon for some friends who were visiting from Tahiti. One of those friends, Carrie Guild, tasted it and cried out, "Maita'i roa ae!" (literally "very good!," figuratively "Out of this world! The best!")—hence the name. It's a mix of rums, curaçao, and lime juice.

Manhattan: The classic and most well-known New York borough cocktail uses a mix of rye, sweet vermouth, and bitters. Classically, Abbott's Bitters were used, but Angostura Bitters are more common now.

metheglin mead: Metheglin is traditional mead (honey wine) with added herbs and/or spices. Some of the most common metheglins are ginger, tea, orange peel, nutmeg, coriander, cinnamon, cloves, and vanilla. Many metheglins were originally employed as folk medicines. The Welsh word for mead is *medd*, and the word "metheglin" derives from *meddyglyn*, a compound of *meddyg*, "healing," and *llyn*, "liquor."

mezcal: Oaxaca, Mexico's agave spirit. Made using a variety of pit-roasted agave plants, mezcal is still produced by the same distillation process that has been used for centuries. Mezcal has rich smoky, earthy tones that set it apart from Jalisco's agave spirit, tequila.

Negroni: Created in the early 1900s in Italy, the Negroni is a classic Italian aperitif made with equal parts gin, sweet vermouth, and Campari.

neutral grain spirit: Colourless and tasteless liquid distilled from grain mash to 95 percent ABV.

New Western dry gin: A style of gin that emerged only in the last few years, following the explosion in the number of distilleries in the Pacific Northwest. Usually contains specialty botanicals only found in the region. The term was coined by Ryan Magarian of Aviation Gin.

Old Fashioned: The Old Fashioned cocktail is one of the original defining classic cocktails. A mix of whiskey (usually bourbon or rye), bitters, and a sugar cube stirred with ice and garnished with a twist of orange or lemon.

Old Pal: A mix of rye, dry vermouth, and Campari. This cocktail first appeared in Harry MacElhone's 1922 book *Harry's ABC of Mixing Cocktails*. He claims the drink was invented by Sparrow Robertson, the then-sporting editor for the *New York Herald*'s office in Paris. It's possible the drink fell out of MacElhone's repertoire by 1927, as it did not appear in his next book, *Barflies and Cocktails*. Instead, in this book, he swapped the rye for bourbon whiskey and renamed the drink "The Boulevardier." The recipe for the Old Pal was published again in Harry Craddock's 1930 cocktail book *The Savoy Cocktail Book*.

Oloroso Sherry: A Spanish fortified wine and one of the sweetest styles of sherry. Its production method allows for heavy oxidization, causing the flavours to be deep and nutty.

orange bitters: Traditionally they are citrusy and slightly bitter, like orange peel.

orgeat syrup: Sweet syrup made from almonds and sugar, with rose water or orange flower water added.

overproof rum: Rum distilled to have a higher ABV, usually in the 60 to 75 percent range. Comes in white and aged styles.

Perlini: A relatively new system consisting of a special pressurized shaker that lets bartenders carbonate any liquid they wish. Created by Perlage (famous for their wine and champagne preservation system).

Peychaud's Bitters: Gentian-based bitters with a lighter body, sweeter taste, and more floral aroma than other bitters that cannot be substituted. First made around 1830 by Antoine Amédée Peychaud, a Creole pharmacist/apothecary from the French colony of Saint-Domingue (now called Haiti), who settled in New Orleans in 1795.

picked: (adjective) A small piece of fruit or vegetable that has a cocktail pick stuck through it.

pimento dram: A rum-based allspice berry liqueur from the Caribbean. Also known as allspice dram.

Pimm's: Pimm's or Pimm's No. 1 (the most available No.) is a gin-based fruit cup or liqueur that was created in 1823 by James Pimm in London for use at his oyster restaurant. Originally there were different "cups," which used different base spirits (for example No. 2 was Scotch-based).

pisco: A brandy that can only be made in Chile or Peru using government-controlled grape varieties and particular distillation methods. Distilled to proof and aged slightly before bottling.

pommeau: A liquor made by mixing apple must (unfermented cider) and aged calvados. Sometimes aged after blending.

PolyScience Smoking Gun: A modern piece of equipment that enables you to cold smoke anything. The traditional method of smoking puts heat to wood chips or other woody substances, which limits what you can smoke because things like liquor cannot have direct heat applied to them for as long as is needed for smoking. The PolyScience Smoking Gun is actually a very simple piece of a equipment: it consists of an electric fan, a small hopper in which to place wood chips or smoking material, and a tube to pump the smoke into the liquid. The fan blows cool air through the hopper, and the lit material inside, and down the tube.

powdered sugar: Finely ground sugar similar to icing sugar.

Prosecco: Generally a dry or extra-dry Italian sparkling wine.

quinquina: A collective name for bitters and fortified wines with quinine (Peruvian Bark) as the main ingredient.

reposado tequila: Tequila that has been aged for six to eighteen months in oak barrels (usually old bourbon barrels).

Rickey: A cocktail similar to a fizz but using lime juice and soda.

rosewater: A by-product of distilling rose petals to extract their oil for perfume. Adds a very floral tone to drinks.

rye whiskey: In the United States, rye whiskey must be made from a mash of at least 51 percent rye, with the rest of the mash made up of corn, barley, etc. In Canada, there is no law on to how much rye needs to be added, so the term Canadian whisky is truer than calling it rye.

Saskatoon berry: Native to the Canadian Prairies and as far west as the coast of British Columbia. Similar to the blueberry in appearance and taste, but with a hint of wild fruit flavour as well.

Sazerac: The Sazerac is a local New Orleans variation of an old-fashioned cognac or whisky cocktail, named for the Sazerac de Forge et Fils brand of cognac that was its original primary ingredient. The drink is made from some combination of cognac or rye whisky, absinthe or Herbsaint, and Peychaud's Bitters; it is distinguished by its preparation method. In 2008, Congress passed a motion naming the Sazerac the official drink of New Orleans, one of the first cocktails to ever get the designation in the US.

schnapps: A strong clear alcohol that can be flavoured with a variety of different ingredients. Popular choices include apple, peppermint, and peach.

shrub: Popular during America's colonial era, the shrub is a simple mixture of fruit, sugar, and vinegar. (In eighteenth-century England, where they originated, shrubs were fortified with liquor such as rum or brandy.)

silver tequila: Silver or blanco tequila is tequila that has been aged no longer than six months in oak. Most producers distil, bring the alcohol content to the required amount, and bottle the tequila without it ever touching oak.

smoking: A new method of adding flavour to a drink using a PolyScience Smoking Gun. Smoking lets bartenders infuse cold smoke into a liquid in a manner of minutes without exposing it to direct heat.

SodaStream Bottle: A simple little piece of equipment that uses a CO_2 tank to infuse the liquid in the pressurized bottle with the gas, carbonating it.

solera: A process for aging liquids in which a succession of containers are filled with product over a series of equal aging intervals (usually each a year). One container is filled for each interval. At the end of the intervals, after the last container is filled, the oldest container is tapped for part of its content, which is bottled. Then that container is refilled from the next oldest container, and that one in succession from the third oldest, down to the youngest container, which is refilled with new product. This procedure is repeated at the end of each aging interval. The transferred product mixes with the older product in the next container.

sour: A classic sour cocktail uses lemon, lime, or any sour citrus to "sour" the drink. Usually a simple mix of spirit, sugar, and sour, sometimes with the addition of egg white.

spiced rum: A classic rum style featuring added and infused spices, such as cinnamon, cloves, and nutmeg.

sprig: A small twig or shoot garnish, most commonly fresh mint, basil, or rosemary.

spritz: A classic style of drink that uses soda or Prosecco as an effervescent element, e.g., Aperol Spritz.

Strega: An Italian herbal liqueur produced since 1860 by the S.A. Distilleria Liquore Strega. Contains about seventy herbal ingredients, including mint, fennel, and saffron, the latter giving it its yellow colour. *Strega* means "witch" in Italian.

sweet vermouth: White (*bianco*) or red (*rosso*) fortified wine, usually 15 to 16 percent alcohol (30–32 proof) and containing up to 15 percent sugar. It is used as an aperitif as well as in slightly sweet cocktails such as the Manhattan.

switchel: A refreshing drink that originated in the Caribbean and is made from ginger, molasses, apple cider vinegar, sugar, and water. It was very popular in the American colonies in the seventeenth century.

swizzle: (verb) To whisk or blend liquor and crushed ice together in a glass.

swizzle: (noun) A cocktail family, usually rum-based drinks with crushed ice, that traditionally was "swizzled" with a small branch that had four to five stalks at the end. Today, you can use a simple stick (such as a chopstick) to achieve the same effect.

Szechuan peppercorns: A common spice in Asian cooking.

Tennessee whiskey: Very similar to bourbon whiskey except made in Tennessee, usually using the sour mash method of fermentation.

tequila blanco: Tequila that has been aged for up to six months in oak barrels (usually old bourbon barrels).

tincture: An alcoholic extract of plant or animal material or a solution with 40 to 60 percent ABV.

Toronto: First published in Robert Vermeire's cocktail book in 1922 as the Fernet Cocktail with the quote, "This cocktail is much appreciated by the Canadians of Toronto." It was later published in David Embury's cocktail book, *The Fine Art of Mixing Drinks*, in 1948 and listed as the Toronto Cocktail. A mix of Canadian whisky, Fernet-Branca, sugar, and Angostura Bitters.

Tuaca Liqueur: A brandy-based liqueur with orange and predominantly vanilla flavours. Originally made in Italy but now manufactured in the US.

turbinado sugar: A style of brown sugar made by spinning molasses in a centrifuge and cooling it into crystals.

Versawhip: Pure, enzymatically treated soy protein that can be hydrated with water and whipped to make a foam.

White Lady: Another classic from Harry McElhone— a refreshing blend of gin, Cointreau, and lemon juice with an optional egg white.

white rum: A common style of rum that has not been aged in a barrel or has been aged for no more than six months and then filtered.

wormwood (*Artemisia absinthium*): An ingredient in absinthe. Also used for flavouring some other spirits and wines, including bitters, vermouth, and Chartreuse.

xanthan gum: A natural, gluten-free carbohydrate produced by fermenting glucose with a bacteria called *Xanthomonas campestris*, which is harmful to plants such as cabbage.

index

acknowledgments

I would love to first thank my wife, Jill, and my little lady, MG, for putting up with the hours, along with my incessant need to work and absorb everything industry-related. A big thank you to my crew for working hard to build the bar into the monolith of cocktails it's become and working even harder when I ask them to—especially Nate, one of the most talented bartenders I have worked with in my career and my long-suffering partner in crime. Another thank you goes to the world's bartenders, brand ambassadors, and friends who have guided me, visited me, and helped the growing cocktail culture in Victoria. And, finally, thank you to the wicked crew who work long hours behind the bar and who made this book worth doing.

—Shawn Soole

To Shawn Soole, Solomon Siegel, and the staff at Pagliacci's restaurant over the years: you have all been fantastic mentors to me. Thank you all for giving me a shot and for becoming some of the best friends I have in this industry.

—Nate Caudle

Nate Caudle (left) and
Shawn Soolc (right)

Shawn Soole & Nate Caudle

Shawn Soole exported himself from Australia to Canada about six and a half years ago when searching for new, greener pastures. He began his career over a decade ago in Brisbane, starting off as a waiter but then finding his passion for the bar far too great. He began bartending and managing at some of the city's most upscale and contemporary cocktail bars, restaurants, and resorts, including Jorge, Vino's, and the only five-star resort in the Whitsundays, Hayman Island. Working in diverse environments, such as restaurants, wine and cocktail bars, flair-tending bars, and boutique beer cafés, has given Shawn insights into every facet of the industry. And he has attempted to experience all aspects of it, from grassroots bartending to executive management. Absorbing all he can about food, wine, beer, and spirits has given his cocktail-making an unusual twist, leading him to combine traditional techniques with cutting-edge ingredients and culinary methods learned from Australia's top chefs. In the years leading up to his leaving for Canada, Shawn organized, judged, and competed in numerous mixology and flair-tending competitions. He won his first Australian Bartenders Guild State Title at the age of twenty-one, was named one of Australia's Best Bartenders, and has had his recipes published in various publications across the country.

After Shawn took over the bar at Clive's Classic Lounge in the Chateau Victoria in 2009, it garnered awards and media attention worldwide. It was twice nominated as Tales of the Cocktail's "World's Best Hotel Bar" (2011, 2012), and Shawn was also nominated as "International Bartender of the Year"—the only Canadian bar and the only Canadian to ever be nominated in any category at Tales of the Cocktail. Recently Shawn embarked on his latest endeavour in Little Jumbo, a small intimate space that showcases the versatility of pairing drinks with food. He has applied all of the things he's learned in his travels and created a new cocktail hub.

Shawn has also appeared on the national TV show *Cityline* and as a speaker at bar shows in Rhode Island, Calgary, and Halifax, and he serves as the MC for many of Canada's cocktail competitions. In addition, he has been featured in *Bar & Beverage Magazine*, *Santé Magazine*, *EAT Magazine*, *About.com*, *Hotel F&B*, *Imbibe*, the *New York Times*, *Whisky Magazine*, and many more local, national, and international publications.

Nate Caudle's fascination with cocktails began with the fun he had entertaining friends and his willingness to play bartender for the night. Taking to it naturally, and enjoying the conversation and good company, Nate chose to pursue this further by enrolling in bar school. He very quickly realized that his new interest had become a passion as he excelled and finished at the top of his class. As a humble reminder of where he started, his diploma still hangs proudly on the wall. His professional bartending career began at the legendary Pagliacci's restaurant in the heart of downtown Victoria. Thrown immediately into the deep end of the service industry, he learned to swim pretty quickly. During his time there, he befriended a fellow enthusiast of the trade. Quite familiar with the bar at his father's restaurant already, Solomon Siegel was making preparations to pioneer a true cocktail renaissance in Victoria. Needing the assistance of a second bartender at Solomon's, he gave Nate the opportunity to advance his skills in the craft and mix in a higher echelon of bartending. Solomon's commitment to providing a quality cocktail drew the attention of a talented Australian bartender, Shawn Soole. Instantly becoming one of Solomon's best regulars and friends, Shawn and Nate soon got acquainted on the other side of the bar. Later down the road, Shawn's and Nate's paths crossed again when Clive's Classic Lounge began garnering enough business to warrant hiring another bartender—and the rest, as they say, is history. Nate kept the team together and joined Shawn at their new place, Little Jumbo.

In his spare time, Nate is an extremely avid enthusiast of exotic animals, and he is still trying to find a way to combine his two passions.